MW01681444

TESTIMONIES OF A WRETCH

Personal Poems From My Journey to Salvation in Jesus Christ

DIANA ROSADO

Two Penny Publishing
1209 SE 21st Avenue
Cape Coral, FL 33990
TwoPennyPublishing.com
info@twopennypublishing.com

ISBN: 978-1-965341-22-3
eBook also available

For permission requests and ordering information, email:
info@twopennypublishing.com

For information about this author, to book an event appearance, or a media interview, please contact the author representative at:
info@twopennypublishing.com

FIRST EDITION

TWO PENNY
PUBLISHING

Two Penny Publishing is a partnership publisher of a variety of genres. We help first-time and seasoned authors share their stories, passion, knowledge, and experiences that help others grow and learn. Please visit our website, TwoPennyPublishing.com if you would like us to consider your manuscript or book idea for publishing.

Disclaimer

This material is intended for mature readers. It may contain themes, language, or subject matter not suitable for younger audiences. Reader discretion is advised.

"A Christian book that actually feels relatable to the common or working class. This book gives a glimpse of Diana's experience as a Christian woman while exposing the good, the bad, and the ugly. The lack of secrecy creates a bond between the reader and the author, thus creating both trust and an engaging experience for the reader. Great job, Diana, and keep up the good work! This is an honorable way to reignite the flame for Jesus, and also invites in unbelievers."

- Ashley Serrano

"Bold and vulnerable, this collection of poems traces the painful journey of surviving abuse with raw honesty and spiritual depth. The author's testimony of faith in Jesus Christ offers strength, comfort, and the promise of restoration. Rooted in the love of Christ, this book offers a sanctuary of hope for anyone seeking healing and peace."

-Jade Creighton

"This book was such a good read! As a Christian who has struggled with her walk, this was encouraging to see the vulnerability of this author in portraying what walking with the Lord can look like. The good and the bad! Definitely recommended for nonbelievers, new believers, and anyone in between!"

- Anne Lee

"An incredibly raw, moving work that looks into the face of abuse and through to the hope on the other side. Both poetry and prose that capture the beautiful highs and lowest lows of the human condition."

- Hannah-Rose Monegro

Dedication

To my children, Rainia, Robert, Ryan, and Royallin: Thank you for the grace, mercy, and forgiveness you have shown me over the past five years. You have all seen things no child should have seen, and you have been through more than most adults. But through it all, God's hand of protection has been over all of you. When I couldn't, God did. Thank you for allowing me to put this book out there and allowing God's work in me to be shared with the world. When I sat you all down and explained that a lot of my ugly will be on display and that people might be mad, you all told me, "Okay, so what?" I was so glad and proud. It has been a joy to watch you all be saved and watch your walk with Jesus Christ. It hasn't always been easy. We have cried, fought, screamed, praised, rejoiced, and united in Christ through it all. So, thank you for your support, kindness, patience, love, and forgiveness as God did His work within me. I cannot leave out my granddaughters, Dior and Sah'raya. It has been a joy to watch you grow. Thank you for all your sassiness, love, and adoration you bring into my life. Our lives would be dull without you both. I love you all dearly.

To my fiancée, Miguel: You came into my life unexpectedly and in an unconventional way, but our story is another book. You have been my muse through this journey. As we started sharing our poems with one another, your lack of condemnation or judgment gave me the courage to keep sharing them with you. You have pointed me back to Jesus through this process. Having you send me scriptures and just telling me how proud you were of me has meant so much to me. You have been patient with me as I went back to these painful events of my life. You pulled me back when my insecurities started to surface. You were gentle, kind, and loving. You have shown me what it is to be cared for mentally, emotionally, and spiritually. Without having to be physical in any way. I am so grateful for what God has done for us individually. It hasn't always been beautiful. It has been messy and ugly, with many trials and tribulations. But God has been faithful and gracious to us. I can't wait to see what He has in store for us as a whole. So, thank you for being such a God-fearing man and loving others with the love of Jesus Christ, including me. It has been a joy to experience you as the new creation in Jesus Christ. I love you. All in!

Preface

This book was first put on my heart in 2016 after I was baptized, but it was just a thought. It was the thought of all that I had been through and exposed to for the glory of God. But I didn't understand what that meant. Hello, I just got baptized. I was just a babe.

As a child, I would always go to a pen and paper to get some relief from the pain I was enduring because I had no one I could truly trust. I don't know why, but in 2016, I started writing out my hurt, anger, pain, and so on. Then I was led to email it to myself.

On December 28, 2023, I met my now fiancé, Miguel. The following day, he said he wanted to read a poem to me. He stated it was from one of his darkest moments. When he read it, my heart broke. I understood the pain. He was waiting for me to be judgmental, but he was surprised by my reaction to seeing the beauty from ashes. After that, he felt comfortable and read another poem to me over the next two days. Then I finally confessed that I, too, wrote poetry, and they were also from my darkest moments in my life. I told him that God had told me to write a book with my poetry years before. He asked me what I was waiting for. Why am I not being obedient to God? That in itself was convicting. I wasn't expecting that, especially since I hadn't read any of my poetry to him yet. Then I told him my reason for not writing the book: I didn't want to offend anyone, and was scared of what people would say and/or do. His reply to that was this: Then they should have treated you better, and who cares what people say. When he said it, it pierced my heart, but not in a bad way. It felt like a piercing from the sword of the Word itself. I didn't receive the words as if Miguel were saying them. I received it like the words were coming from the Holy Spirit that dwells within Miguel. It was the realization of my disobedience, and it reminded me of what the disciple Paul said in Galatians 1:10.

For am I now seeking the approval of man, or of God? Or am I trying to please man? If I were still trying to please man, I would not be a servant of Christ. (ESV)

After repenting and thanking Miguel for being a willing vessel of our Lord Jesus Christ, I started to write the book God put on my heart seven years earlier.

Table of Contents

Part One: My Life Before Jesus Christ 1

Part Two: My Confessions as a Babe in Christ 11

Part Three: My Addictions... 21

Part Four: My Failed Earthly Marriage............................. 43

Part Five: My Identity in Jesus Christ................................ 57

Part Six: My Testimony 69

Part Seven: Prayers.. 97

A Special Letter to You. The Reader.................................117

Letters to My Children and Grandchildren..................... 121

Letter to Myself 135

Acknowledgements 147

About the Author.. 151

1

MY LIFE BEFORE JESUS CHRIST

The woman I was before Jesus has become extremely hard to see or remember. Praise God! A woman scorned is an understatement. I was full of hurt, pain, lust, guilt, vengeance, grudges, anger, malice, unforgiveness, selfishness, greed, pride, hate, and everything that evil creates. These poems touch on some of those things and show a lot of my ugliness.

I was a very lustful woman. I have had multiple abortions. I used to partake in getting high, popping pills, and drinking alcohol. I fought excessively with the intention or thought of harming people. I had no compassion, no remorse, no emotion. I was a hollow, empty shell of flesh. I literally was the definition of the *Walking Dead*. I was a wicked woman, and apart from God, that is what I will always be.

As I write this, I cannot believe I used to be this woman. I am no longer this woman but a daughter of the Most High God! I am a new creation.

Therefore, if anyone is in Christ, he is a new creation. The old has passed away; behold, the new has come.

2 Corinthians 5:17

I wanted to show you all who I was in the flesh and who I was before Jesus, so you can see the work the Lord has done in me. I was blind, deaf, and had a heart of stone, but Jesus gave me eyes to see and ears to hear.

"But blessed are your eyes, for they see, and your ears, for they hear. For truly, I say to you, many prophets and righteous people longed to see what you see, and did not see it, and to hear what you hear, and did not hear it."

Matthew 13:16-17

He has also turned my heart of stone into a heart of flesh.

I will sprinkle clean water on you, and you shall be clean from all your uncleannesses, and from all your idols I will cleanse you. And I will give you a new heart, and a new spirit I will put within you. And I will remove the heart of stone from your flesh and give you a heart of flesh. And I will put my Spirit within you, and cause you to walk in my statutes and be careful to obey my rules.

Ezekiel 36:25-27

Because of these things, I can come to you all with the truths of this previous version of myself. I am not ashamed; I have no pride, and it is all for God to get the Glory!

I Think It Is Time To Run

The kids are asleep, and he
is out with the guys.

It's safe for me to sit here and cry.

I cannot cry in front of him;
it makes him upset.

I cannot seem to do anything right.

I cook, clean, and take care of the kids.

But he always finds a flaw, and
BOOM, another fight.

From a busted nose and bruises
on my body to black eyes.

I hope he does not come home
high and drunk again tonight.

Oh no, he is wasted; let me
pretend to be asleep…

"911, what is the emergency?"

Jesus? No, Thank You!

Oh gosh, here we go again.

Mami wakes us all up at 7:00 am.

To sit at church from dusk to dawn.

The only thing I do is sing, and then the
rest of the time is spent in yawns.

My siblings and I are always getting into fights,

And then here comes Mami with her nails pinching our skin tight.

Man, I loved that old lady.

But man, when it comes to her Jesus, she gets a little hasty.

I always watch her on her knees daily.

From morning to night, constantly praying.

She would name all her children and
grandchildren, down to the baby.

I heard my name a few times, but not as
much as my sister and aunt.

I will not mention names, but they know who they are.

As I got older and watched my family
become more broken and divided,

It was hard to have hope for this Jesus, and I just decided…

Jesus? No, thank you, I will take my chances out there.

Oh, He's Cute, I Like

I remember the first time we locked eyes.
We didn't talk, but always looked at each
other while he was out with the guys.

I desired him and needed
    to make a move.

I was trying to find the perfect time
to speak to him; I felt like a fool.

    One night, I decided to get a
    bottle; I hadn't seen him all day.

My sister and I were drunk,
and then she stepped away.
I was sitting in front of the
building, and here he comes.

    "Oh, he is so cute, tall,
    dark, and has those lips."

He sees me and smiles, and
notices I am drunk.

It was like we were both waiting
for this opportunity.
We started flirting, and then we
scheduled a day to sleep together.

I thought he was bluffing, but
    I knew I was down for whatever.

The day came, and he had
a girl sitting on him.

I didn't care; I didn't want a man.

I just wanted to take him for a spin.

He apologized later that night, and we
just set up another day to get it in.

The day came, and he had
everything worked out.

And what happened next was
amazing, without a doubt.
We became friends with
benefits instantly.

And within a month, he almost
became my baby daddy.

But drinking forced a miscarriage.

We never stopped, and I did not care
if he had a family; he wasn't married.

Two years of this and we fell in love.

He had a key to my crib and would come
and go while the kids were sleeping.

One miscarriage, two abortions,
one of which was twins.

He got locked up, and I was unaware;
I thought he was over me.

I'm not waiting for anybody;
on to the next.

I had a guy over within the next
two weeks; he whistled, and I knew
he was coming up the stairs.

I told my sister to send him
into the bathroom while I was
showering for the next dude.

I told him I had company,
and he had to leave.

He was pissed, but what can he say?
    He can go home to his girl
    and their children.

I did me, and he was back at the
crib the very next morning.

We talked, we cried, and
    we said our goodbyes.

He still loves me to this day, and
we chat from time to time.
        But we knew we just fell in
        love at the wrong time.

I traded him for the man
from the night before.

        That man now knows
        me as his ex-wife.

Three Strikes, I Should Have Been Out

I remember it like it was yesterday.

I got in trouble for having friends
over without permission.

I was around 11 years old and
got smacked by my dad.

I go into the bathroom;
I am over all this crap.

I was tired of never being
able to do anything but
having to do everything.

I was tired of my dad not
knowing the truth.

I was tired of this life and all the
stuff I had already been through.

Without thinking, I opened
the medicine cabinet.

I am going to take all these pills.

I do not remember the names, but I
know they belonged to my stepmother.

I counted eighty-nine pills and felt fine.
Ugh.

Two hours later, I was in the ER because
the whites of my eyes turned yellow.

I stayed for a week under psych watch.

    Am I really still alive?

Years go by, and the thoughts
of killing myself still linger.

But today's actions came
after the thought.

He came home mad, so we got into a
fight and he beat the crap out of me.

I went into my safe place to
do it, the bathroom.
I grabbed the first thing
    I saw and drank it.

The liquid got foamy and now
lingered in my mouth.
That dark brown bottle to heal wounds
was not healing my unseen scars.

I started throwing up and waited for
any sign that it worked this time.

The clock ticked by, and I
was still throwing up.

    And then I felt my baby kick
    and broke down crying.

I was here trying to take my life,
forgetting that one was growing inside.

More years have passed by.

Now, here I am, drinking to
drown the voices and thoughts.

Never chased the alcohol with any
juice; I might have taken a pill or two.

Ecstasy was the pill of my choice;
what a beautiful combination.

The drinks helped so much. It left
me without the ability to think.

I'm broke;
cheers to that.

I'm numb with no emotions;
cheers to that.

I'm lost and there's no way out;
cheers to that.

I'm unworthy;
cheers to that.

I'm useless;
cheers to that.

I'm.................

Being woken up by my ex-
husband because I had passed
out and vomited everywhere.

Third attempt of suicide on my
life. Can I get anything right?

Isn't the rule three strikes and you're out?

2

MY CONFESSIONS AS A BABE IN CHRIST

I was saved in 2015 at a church in Manhattan, New York, called Hillsong. I attended Hillsong while they were still renting out a space on Sunday mornings from a nightclub. I liked the idea of worshiping and meeting the Lord in a place that was full of sin the night before. I felt right at home. I even followed them when they moved to 34th Street. The following year, in 2016, I was baptized by Hillsong.

Once I was baptized, I assumed that life would get better and be much easier. I thought all I had to do was pray and God would hear and answer. I saw God as a genie. Boy, was I wrong! I would soon learn that giving my life to Jesus Christ would be the hardest thing I have ever done. To be chosen to be a living sacrifice for the Lord has been absolutely the most rewarding thing I have ever had the privilege to do.

I appeal to you therefore, brothers, by the mercies of God, to present your bodies as a living sacrifice, holy and acceptable to God, which is your spiritual worship.

Romans 12:1

In this section, you will see me struggling with understanding how prayer works, who God is, and where it leaves me. I struggled with this for an exceedingly long time. I just learned how to trust and lean on Jesus in 2021. This understanding only came from me being in God's Word and being among like-minded Christian brothers and sisters.

Iron sharpens iron, and one man sharpens another.

Proverbs 27:17

Community is a necessity on this journey! We were not meant to walk this walk alone. First, walk with Jesus. Secondly, surround yourself with a community that will keep you accountable and give you Biblical corrections, as well as those willing to exchange burdens with you.

Brothers, if anyone is caught in any transgression, you who are spiritual should restore him in a spirit of gentleness. Keep watch on yourself, lest you too be tempted. Bear one another's burdens, and so fulfill the law of Christ.

Galatians 6:1-2

GOD, WHY?

Before we were born, our
story was already written.

But why, God, did mine have
to be a story of forgiveness?

To forgive those who sexually, mentally,
physically, and emotionally abused me?

They broke my spirit, mind, and
heart, and took my inner beauty.

Like a thief in the night, they took
my soul and all my innocence.

Now, I'm an empty body with
a hardened heart and memories
that have taken my sanity.

I have been diagnosed with
depression, PTSD, and OCD.

While these people who broke
me walk around like they never
did these things to me.

Father, I hated You for a very long time;
I ask, why have You forsaken me?

Now, I see that it wasn't You who
sent these things to happen to me.

You cried and stood over me while
Your child endured this pain.

You never left me; You just kept filling
me with Your strength and glory.

You waited for me to get on my
knees and tell You my story.

You waited for me to cry in prayer
with my broken heart and soul.

You waited for me to declare I was Your
child and ready to be made whole.

So, I came to You with my worries,
fears, tears, and brokenness.

Giving You my broken heart, which is
all You have ever wanted me to give.

You have restored my hope,
faith, and love for You.

So even when I ask God, why me?

I also give you all the glory and say
thank You, Father, for choosing me!

Have You Forgotten Me?

I have cried for Your help for my daughter.

I have cried for You to heal my son.

I have cried for You to take my marriage into Your hands.

I have cried and given You my broken heart and myself.

I have cried for You to forgive me for my
sins; I have cried for Your love.

I have cried for You to protect my home
and family from our enemies.

I have cried for Your strength, grace, faith, wisdom, and guidance.

I have cried for You to build my faith.

I have given You my life and was reborn.

I have cried in the dark, in the shower, in my bed, on
the streets, and have done this while on my knees.

Father, have You forgotten me?

Where Are You?

You promised to be strong for me.

Yet, I'm weaker than I have ever been.

You promised to carry me when I can't walk.

Yet, I'm paralyzed and haven't gone anywhere.

You promised to forgive me.

Yet, I felt like I was being punished.

You promised to love me unconditionally.

Yet, I'm feeling unloved and alone.

You promised to never forsake me.

So, why am I in this darkness?

Where's Your strength?

Where's Your love?

Where's my Savior?

Where are you?

Father Speak

Father, why has my faith dwindled?

Why can I not get closer to You?

I'm losing this fight between
my spirit and my flesh.

My energy and will to seek
You has obliterated.

My mind is trapped in its mental illness.

Father, help me find You!

Please bring back and restore my faith in
You that this world has taken from me.

Please bring back the light in my heart
so my spirit can shine once more.

Please, Father, I beg You to
remove these chains.

I am drowning.

Please, Father, hear my cries for
Your mercy to be poured upon me.

Father, where are You?
Can You hear me?

My heart has hardened, and I need
Your unconditional love to soften it.

Remove these evil thoughts concerning
You from this mind of mine.

Remove this pain from my
heart against You.

Father, are You there? Father?

Father, please answer me!

Father, save me from myself.

Father, please answer me!

Father, save my soul.

Father, please answer me!

Father, please, please, please!

Restore my faith!

Father!?

Your Storm

Father, this storm that
I'm in has been the worst
I have ever seen.

From a daughter who has
become a chronic runaway.

A son who is suffering from
an incurable disease.

And another son who was just
diagnosed with ADHD.

But the storm doesn't
stop there!

Let's add my depression,
PTSD, and OCD.

My marriage is getting hit
hard by all these elements.

This storm has me drowning
in a dark whirlpool.

I have realized this storm
is NOT my storm.

I am fighting a fight that
You have already won!

So I stopped driving this
boat and went to the back
of it to awaken You.

Father, I ask that You
take the wheel and speak
into this storm.

For You and only You do
the winds and rains listen.

For You are the only
one powerful enough
to calm this storm.

I will no longer look through
the darkness to see the light.

I am now on my knees,
speaking to the source
of the light.

Father, take control of
this wheel and speak
into this storm.

DEAR GOD

I'm calling on You to revive me and give me
the strength I need to care for my family.

You know I love them, but keeping
everything together can be overwhelming.

Teach me ways to better relate to my
family and to guide them as I should.

Comfort me, guide me, and give me
the strength I need to keep going.

Heavenly Father, I know You
have a plan for my child.

I thank You and praise You for allowing
me the gift of being his/her mother.

I am frustrated because I want
to see the fruits of my labor.

WOE IS ME! Please forgive
me for neglecting what You
did on that cross for me.

It was Your blood that You spilled
on that cross that will bring forth
the fruit of my children.

Because they are Your children first.

Lord, please give me the patience
to continue being obedient to Your
words in raising Your children.

3 MY ADDICTIONS

I used to be addicted to many things: Cigarettes, pills, sex, alcohol, and even words of affirmation. Each addiction came with its own chains and invisible strings. As I sit and write this chapter, I cannot believe my addictions started at the early age of nine years old. Each poem is an insight into the pain, confusion, anger, and so much more I experienced. I didn't see any other way to share these poems except for them to be raw, real, and blunt. I also saw no need to mention names, for the fact that I have already forgiven those who hurt me. I'm not going to lie and say I did not struggle going back to those moments in my life. However, the only way for this to be authentic was to revisit the most traumatic memories that almost destroyed me. It has been very therapeutic and healing to share this, knowing that it might encourage others to share their stories and break their silence.

I pray that you don't feel any pity for me or hate towards those who hurt me. They are also God's creations, and there is no one too far gone for the salvation of Jesus Christ. I would ask that you come alongside me and pray for them and every lost sheep out there. You do not need to know their names; God already knows who they are. Thank you in advance for your prayers.

First of all, then, I urge that supplications, prayers, intercessions, and thanksgivings be made for all people, for kings and all who are in high positions, that we may lead a peaceful and quiet life, godly and dignified in every way. This is good, and it is pleasing in the sight of God our Savior, who desires all people to be saved and to come to the knowledge of the truth. For there is one God, and there is one mediator between God and men, the man Christ Jesus, who gave himself as a ransom for all, which is the testimony given at the proper time.

1 Timothy 2:1-6

Just a Girl Living in a Grown-Up World

At nine years old,
    I had my first sexual experience.

Groggy and half asleep, I feel someone
standing over me as I lie in bed.

He removed my comforter and
started touching my chest.

I intuitively knew who it was and
heard his breathing pick up speed.

I became paralyzed, and I knew it was
wrong, but I had trouble understanding.

I stayed stiff as a board, fake sleeping.

Against better judgment, my fear forces
one of my eyes to crack open.

It's pitch black, and he was so focused
on what he was doing to notice.

I see him rubbing his privates, and
    all I can say is God, please no.

He pulls his basketball shorts down,
and now he's fully exposed.

His hands move from my chest to
my lips and part them open.

I silently watch through my cracked-open eyelids.

His penis moved closer to my
mouth, and before I knew it…

My eyes flew wide open.

He's frozen like a statue
as our eyes connect.

But it doesn't stop him; a few
seconds, and it starts up again.

He places his finger over his lips,

Shhhhhh!

Out of fear, I go along with it.

He finishes and puts his shorts
back on, and that was it for him.

He gently covers me back up and
just walks away, licking his lips.

Me on the other hand…

I lay in confusion.

I lay paralyzed.

I lay in shock.

I lay in shame.

I lay in a daze.

I lay while feeling the
remains of his DNA.

I lay and lay, in numbness of
that moment in time.

It felt like forever before I felt
safe enough to muster up the
courage to pull myself up.

I go straight to the bathroom to
remove every trace of him from me.

I shake nervously back to my bed,
    still in disbelief.

Tears ran quietly down my cheeks.

Little did I know this would become
part of my nightly bedtime routine.

At least twice a week for a
few weeks? Months?

    I lost count.

I got used to it, but one day
    I was finally fed up.

I spoke up and reported it,
but was quickly silenced.

And this was from those who were
supposed to care for and protect me.

I was instructed not to tell
my dad about any of it.

But here I am, thirty-nine years
later, breaking my silence.

That night opened my appetite for
sex, sexual immorality, and lust.

Unbeknownst to me, it would also
be the root of my other addictions.

Porn, drugs, pills, alcohol, and men.

That night, my innocence was
stolen, my worth diminished,
and my mind confused.

That night, my mind
connected love to sex.

All because of a man whose
demons weren't satisfied by a
girlfriend he already had.

That night opened years of
trauma I struggled with and
doors I couldn't close.

This was until I met my Lord
and Savior, Jesus Christ.

Jesus came into my life and
cracked open my stony heart.

He took all of my grudges, hate,
hurt, pain, and unforgiveness.

He replaced it with peace,
mercy, grace, forgiveness, and
unconditional love for me.

My identity changed from dirty shame
to clean and washed by His blood.

This transformation covered me with the
goodness, beauty, and truth of Jesus.

Now I'm set free.

Dad, please forgive me for all
these years of secrecy.

It's Just Sex

From the age of nine, I
learned to use my body.

I had boys in my school buying
me candy and food.

My body gave me gifts, attention,
    and a mind full of lust.

I had my first boyfriend
at the age of eleven.

He was such a sweet, kind, loving boy.

He was unaware of my trauma
and all my brokenness.

We loved each other, well, as
good as children could love.

But I didn't love him enough to open
up about the molestation at home.

His love wasn't enough, and my love
for him was overpowered by my lust.

    I wanted more than
    what he could give.

I wanted more attention, more
gifts, more this, and more that.

But the problem was I wanted
it from more guys.

I didn't care; I didn't have a type.

This caused my boyfriend so
much hurt, so I had to prove to
him I really did love him.

So, I gave him something no one ever
had….My virginity at the age of twelve.

But that relationship didn't last long.

I broke it off three months
later; it wasn't him at all.

> I grew up too fast, and so
> what? It was just sex.

"Just sex" made me a teen mother of two
children before the age of eighteen.

"Just sex" led me into a domestic
violence relationship.

"Just sex" was like eating an appetizer,
never fully being satisfied.

"Just sex" left me with shame and
guilt, so I covered it up with more.

"Just sex" put my life and health at risk.

"Just sex" made me an
empty shell because…

IT IS NOT JUST SEX!

For the Word of God says:

"But from the beginning of creation, 'God made them male and female.' 'Therefore, a man shall leave his father and mother and hold fast to his wife, and the two shall become one flesh.' So they are no longer two but one flesh. What therefore God has joined together, let not man separate."

Mark 10:6-9

Sex is a blessing and a
gift from the Lord.

To be enjoyed by those He
has joined together under His
covenant of marriage.

The enemy had me confused
between love and lust.

The enemy did his job well of
lying and deceiving me.

The lust of this world is what
makes sex "just sex."

But sex in marriage is the joining of
two people and them becoming one.

Sex is a worship unto the Lord as a
covenant under His law and union.

The enemy did everything to keep me
in the bed of sin outside of marriage.

He is also doing everything to
keep those in marriage out of that
covenantal bed under God.

It's a beautiful and intimate
exchange that will not leave you
in shame or full of regret.

It will leave you satisfied, and it will
bring glory and praise to the Lord.

Good try, Satan; Jesus is victorious
over you...YET AGAIN!

Affirmations? Yes, Please

I did not grow up in a home
that gave me affirmation.

A lot of abuse and negativity gave
me a mindset of isolation.

I started to grow into my
young lady's body.

Guys of all ages started to notice
me, and I became very cocky.

My body attracted the sweet
words of lust and fake promises.

Beautiful daydreams, lies, and every
other wicked, lustful accomplice.

My head was so full of air and
grew bigger and bigger, leaving
no room for thinking.

Without thoughts came stupidity,
and allowing these men to use me.

For a free fill of my body, a kiss,
and, ultimately, my virginity.

All I had going for myself was
a big butt and double D's.

I didn't mind since my body didn't
belong to me in the first place.

Remember, at home, he owned it,
but outside, I have all the say.

I got things like money, food, and gifts,
and I didn't have to open my legs.

This was a sweet deal! This was
how you show "love" anyway.

I kept trying to convince myself
that as long as I didn't sleep
with them, I was good.

Being thirteen and having only slept
with one guy was great in the hood.

This mindset followed me into my
teenage and early adult years.

Fifteen and pregnant.

Seventeen and pregnant.

Nineteen and pregnant,
miscarriage, that was a close one.

Twenty and pregnant, nope, not
this time, abortion for this one.

Twenty and pregnant, what the hell!

I guess it's okay; it's from the same
guy who beats the crap out of me.

Twenty-one and now a single parent of
three, and hiding from their father.

Alcohol and affirmations to drown
the pain of this scary place.

This led to more men and more
clinics to hide my shame.

More abortions, miscarriages, a
fallen marriage, then I realized...

> I am addicted to words
> of affirmation, and it has
> a hard grip on me.

Being addicted to words is crazy!

It would be me to take
things to the extreme.

How do I break this addiction, and is
there even a way I could be set free?

I got my answer in 2015.

I was a murderer of eight
children, sentenced to death for
eternity due to all my sins.

I walked into a nightclub that
was converted into a sanctuary
for Sunday Church service.

> I lifted my hands and repented and
> received the free gift of salvation.

I felt His spiritual hands wrap around
me and instantly started sobbing.

As if every tear that dropped
represented freedom.

I felt the presence of the Holy Spirit and soon
felt the absence of the heaviness I was carrying.

I walked in full of bondage, brokenness,
and loss, and I was spiritually dead.

I left free, full of joy, restored, and reborn.

I was brought to life by the blood of Jesus
Christ at a place where sinners play.

It shows the power and authority of
Jesus and how He meets you in the
darkest and dirtiest of places.

There is no place Jesus cannot enter, and I'm glad
it was my heart He broke into with His grace.

Jesus replaced the many words of
affirmation this world offers.

With one word, He restored my worth, and
that is when He called me daughter.

The Bottom of the Bottle

Just got picked up by a person from
the domestic violence hotline.

I was placed in a ten-day placement
while they did their investigation.

I met some people who
seemed cool and chill.

I had already purchased two gallons
of Bacardi for the ten-day stay.

I wonder if they want to hang
out and have a drink.

I had so much fun and did things
I would have never done sober.

> Then I realized it was my first
> time alone as an adult; I'm free!

No parents, no abuser, no
rules, and no limits.

> Little did I know that the Jezebel
> spirit was about to take over me.

The bottle became my best friend
and my biggest cheerleader.

That liquid courage took me
into the darkness, and Satan
became my ringleader.

I had no fear, no remorse, no worry, no
cares when Paul Mason came into play.

That Hennessy and Bacardi were
okay, but that Long Island Iced Tea
turned me into a drunken cliché.

Fun, freedom, my life, my way, parties,
sex, pills, and puffs of the Mary-Jane.

I wasn't hurting anyone; I partied in
my home or the homes of my family.

Yes, I was a single mother of
three; they're young, and they
will never remember this.

So what if I was sleeping with
a man who had a family?

No one cared when they hurt me,
plus they aren't even married.

We "love" each other, and we feed
each other's sexual appetite without
the strings of a relationship.

Sneaking around is part of the
excitement until the emotional
abortion clinic trips.

I killed for the thrill of this
new kind of sexual high.

Two years of that adventure,
now I'm over it.

Time for a new adventure with this
new man who has entered the scene.

More drinking and flirting, and
we are quickly in the sheets.

Another pregnancy and him
begging me to get rid of it.

"I'm too young to be a dad,"
was what he said.

I know that wasn't the truth; he just
saw me as another girl to "smash."

Within the year, another abortion,
but at least this time we are married.

I started to sober up, and the knowledge
of all my mistakes started to surface.

Here comes the guilt, shame,
and truth that my children
will remember everything.

I felt like the bottom of
that alcohol bottle.

Transparent, empty, and heading
straight for the trash.

I was about to throw in the towel
when I encountered the Lord.

Now saved and redeemed
and no longer ashamed.

This was only possible when I said
Jesus, and His name I proclaimed.

July 30, 2024, marked three years free
of alcohol and all its toxic friends.

Indwelled by the Holy Spirit,
the Jezebel spirit fled.

God's work is currently still
healing and sustaining me.

But my sinful lifestyle has
caused a ripple effect.

My kids got caught up in
all my consequences.

I bled my trauma on them,
and it has now created their
own trauma to deal with.

Now, my family is united and connected
by the blood of Jesus Christ.

For God has pierced each of our hearts
by His Word, also known as a sword.

AS FOR ME AND MY FAMILY,
WE WILL SERVE THE LORD!

Oh, That Good Old Cancer Stick

I thought it would be cool
to try a cigarette.

My dad and stepmother smoke,
so I had easy access to it.

I grabbed one and went to the
East River on the FDR Drive.

Cig in one hand, lighter in the other.

I spark the lighter and inhale.

Instantly, I started choking,
but didn't care.

There I was at the age of eleven,
smoking a non-menthol cancer stick.

My curiosity wasn't satisfied,
so I tried again.

I'm a perfectionist and a little
bit of a control freak.

I don't give up easily, even when I
know something is bad for me.

I already felt grown, so who
was going to stop me?

It was time to try my dad's brand.

Newport shorts, packaged in a green
box stating they were menthol.

Oh, these are smoother; I
think I like these more.

BOOM! Now I'm addicted to
this menthol-flavored nicotine.

I would take a cigarette
for my daily puff at a
secret hiding place.

The nights I stayed at
Mami's house, I would
find her secret stash…

I smoked any brand as
long as it was menthol.

It didn't matter if they were
long, short, fresh, or stale.

By the age of twelve, I was a pro
and smoking more and more.

What I thought was a cool
fashion statement became one
of my hardest strongholds.

This choice left me with
weak lungs, struggles with
weight, a body full of nicotine
toxins, and a missing tooth.

Twenty-five years of
slavery to that cancer stick
and all its bad habits.

I've tried to quit several times.

Only to meet failure and
defeat with thoughts of a
cigarette entrapment.

I was held down by
this addiction for a
quarter of a century.

Then the Word of
God said to me,

I can do all things through
him who strengthens me.

Philippians 4:13

Now, three years
clean and set free.

Only by the strength and
power of the Trinity.

You've done it again!

Thank you, Abba, Father, Jesus,
Son of God, and the Holy
Spirit that dwells within me.

4

MY FAILED EARTHLY MARRIAGE

December 1, 2010, was the day I got married. We were both unsaved, and I proposed to him. We did love each other, or we thought we did. We also got married for tax reasons and because we wanted a child. It wasn't all horrible, but I cried more than I laughed or smiled. Twelve years of him sleeping, flirting, and chatting with other women caused me to feel unworthy, unlovable, depressed, and vengeful. There was infidelity on both sides. I am not blaming my failed marriage solely on my ex-husband. We both had a role in it, and both caused each other pain.

This marriage started worldly. It was based on money, sex, and having a good time. However, when I was saved in 2015, I started to see marriage through the eyes of Jesus. I prayed for this marriage for six years. The more I prayed, the more things went downhill. I was no longer going to stay in a marriage that was full of greed, adultery, mental, emotional, and verbal abuse. In 2021, we separated (for the hundredth time), and the divorce was finalized in March, 2022. It was a very difficult decision and took a lot of prayer. I had to analyze every aspect of what this divorce would mean for both me and my children. My oldest three children were okay with it (which should have been a sign of how broken this marriage really was), but I knew the daughter we shared together would take it hard. The other children endured years of watching and hearing us argue, bicker, yell, and much more.

I learned two things in this worldly marriage. First, if you are not saved and don't know Jesus, you do not know love, so receiving and showing love is not in you because God is love. The Bible says:

> *Beloved, let us love one another, for love is from God, and whoever loves has been born of God and knows God. Anyone who does not love does not know God, because God is love.*
>
> 1 John 4:7-8

God is not only love, but He is the creator of love.

Secondly, and this might bother some Christians, if your marriage ended in divorce, it was not joined together by God. This is a promise from the Lord.

> *"'Therefore a man shall leave his father and mother and hold fast to his wife, and the two shall become one flesh.' So they are no longer two but one flesh. What therefore God has joined together, let not man separate."*
>
> Mark 10: 7-9

The promise said no man can part, not even the two people in the marriage, and God will never separate a marriage covenant. I know this is a hard pill of revelation for us Christians to take. I took what was Holy and sacred to God and used it for my worldly and sinful gain, but I have been forgiven and restored from this sin. There is nothing too big or small for God to forgive, restore, redeem, and/or make new.

I Loved You Through It All

I'm just not meant to be loved.

Unwanted trash is how I'm
treated by those I love.

This is how I used to think and
feel, but I know better now.

I am meant to be loved
because GOD loves me.

I am a masterpiece because He
created me through His eyes.

I'm a great woman, wife, mother,
friend, daughter, and sister.

I have a kind, loving, forgiving,
and generous heart.

I have been there with you
through thick and thin.

I stood by you when life was against you.

I cared for you when you were sick.

I kept you fed, clothed, and
built a home for us.

I had your back even though you
disrespected, broke, betrayed,
and hurt me and our family.

I'm the glue that kept us together, and
I always put you and the kids first.

I didn't ask for much but
your time and love.

You should have been a role model and
provider and given your family attention.

All these things I was supposed
to get as your wife.

There is nothing wrong with me.

My only failure I had was
trying to save my husband from
a life of sin and adultery.

Am I the Problem?

What's wrong with me?

Abused since I was a child, but the last
eight years have been the most painful.

My heart was cold due to abuse,
but you came into my life, and
the ice chipped away.

Only for you to have it, take it, bend,
break, stomp, and destroy it.

I trusted you with the only
thing I had left to give.

Constantly forgiving you and building
what you tore down repeatedly.

From inappropriate pictures of
girls to sleeping with them.

From chat rooms to staircases.

From MySpace to Facebook.

From the courthouse for
marriage to divorce.

Am I the problem?

I Can't Be

I am the woman you want
and need, but I will never
be the woman you seek.

I'm not and will never be
one of those Lowa girls
you are so interested in.

So, I let you go.

I pray you find what you are
looking for and that God
keeps you from harm.

May God place His hands on
your life and cover you with
the blood of Jesus Christ.

Only God knows how
much this is hurting me.

I honestly just want you
to be happy, and I pray
for your health.

I can't be the woman who
treats you like your mom.

I can't be that woman
whose heart you can
continuously break.

I can't be that woman
full of hate and anger.

I can't and I won't.

I can't be the woman
you want me to be.

I can't smoke; I need to
be alive for my kids.

I can't be the woman
many men slept with.

I can't be your doormat
anymore.

I gave you all I had to offer, but
I see it will never be enough.

I have been praying for God
to fix this marriage because
I didn't want to fail again.

There comes a time when
enough is enough.

Sometimes what you want isn't
what God had for you, but
He allowed you to choose.

I was the right woman for the
wrong man, and that's okay.

I was trying to fit into a
puzzle I never belonged to.

No matter how much you
care for and love a person,

If that isn't who God created
for you, He will remove them.

So, with that said…

God will always give you
what you need and not
necessarily what you want.

I love you. Goodbye.

I Can't Make You

He was living it up.

I see and understand now.

I can't save you from temptation.

I can't make you healthier.

I can't make you love me.

I can't make you whole.

I can't make you a better husband.

I can't make you a better man.

I can't make you want this marriage.

I can't make you believe in God.

Only you can want to change
with God's helping hands.

I am not your savior; that power
only comes from Jesus Christ.

Let the Games Begin: Player Two Just Stepped In

I'm tired of looking stupid
and letting you back in.

Now it's my turn to cause
the same hurt and pain.

Let's call up my go-to; he
never tells me no.

He's on his way and ready to play.

We played adult wrestling and
went our separate ways.

My husband was so caught up in his
own sin that he never noticed mine.

> Okay, he cheated again; player
> two, you're up; take your place.

I called my backup, and
we met at a hotel.

My husband doesn't know I
was out because he just started
working overnight.

Ugh, here he goes cheating again.

> I can't do this anymore;
> do I kick him out?

I'm trying to be a better person now
that I have been recently saved.

Let me go hang out with
some friends at a bar.

Dang, I'm drunk and recently
separated from my husband.

A guy pulled me in, we kissed, and
noticed we needed to run to the store.

We purchased some condoms
and some wraps for him.

I put my life on the line for a drunken
temporary scratch for my current itch.

We go a few rounds and
then reality sets in.

Oh, God, please forgive me; wait, this
doesn't count; we are not even together.

The guilt set in, and two months
later, my husband and I tried again.

I am never telling him this; I'm
taking that to my grave.

I will deny it with all I have.

I'm such a hypocrite; oh, well, I'm
forgiven because I'm saved.

I went to a mega church, so no
discipleship was offered.

I had no knowledge or wisdom
on what true salvation meant.

All I know is now I am holding
on to this lie and feel the
heaviness of the regret.

God, what have I done, and
why am I feeling this way?

I never felt this after I played
the revenge game.

Years later, I would understand
the word *conviction.*

That remorse that conviction brings
is a whole other level of affliction.

Now I do everything I can
to not feel it willingly.

But there's a time the Holy Spirit
convicts me for the sake of humility.

I Gave Up

After twelve years of forcing
this union, I gave up.

I gave up crying at night, wondering
what time he was coming home.

I gave up stressing about who he was
chatting and flirting with beside me.

I gave up wanting to please him, and
sleeping next to him caused me anxiety.

I gave up waiting for him
to appreciate me.

I gave up asking him to love
me and see me for me.

I gave up caring about his whereabouts.

I gave up waiting up at night
and mentally hurting myself.

I gave up secretly crying in the shower.

I gave up all the stress and misery
this "marriage" brings me.

I gave up eating crumbs
and being starved.

I gave up on you, so I can
finally start loving myself.

5

MY IDENTITY IN JESUS CHRIST

Then God said, "Let us make man in our image, after our likeness. And let them have dominion over the fish of the sea and over the birds of the heavens and over the livestock and over all the earth and over every creeping thing that creeps on the earth."

Genesis 1:26

He is the image of the invisible God, the firstborn of all creation. For by him all things were created, in heaven and on earth, visible and invisible, whether thrones or dominions or rulers or authorities—all things were created through him and for him. And he is before all things, and in him all things hold together.

Colossians 1:15-17

The above verses show where we get our image and identity from. We were all created in the likeness of the Trinity. Below are some definitions of likeness from the Oxford Languages:

1. The fact or quality of being alike; resemblance.
2. The semblance, guise, or outward appearance of.
3. A portrait or representation.

We are all these definitions and much more when it comes to the likeness of God. But it's not just Abba, Father. Reread what Genesis 1:26 says. Let us create them in our image. You were not just created in the image of God but the image of Jesus, the Son, and the Holy Spirit. I never understood this when I first started my Christian walk. But the more I walked, the more I got a glimpse of who I was in my flesh and who God was, in His holiness.

It took me years to see my identity in Jesus. For the first twenty-nine years of my life, my identity was in men, drugs, alcohol, and words of affirmation. Then God started putting a "mirror" in front of me and showing me all my flaws, ugliness, pain, brokenness, etc. I did not like that "mirror!" I still don't like that "mirror." I call it the mirror of God's truths. That mirror exposed every lie the enemy has ever told me. With this new tool and the wisdom God was instilling within me, I began to let go of what I had been taught by the world and allowed God to reteach me and train me in His truth and commands. Little by little, the reflection in the mirror started changing. I was a slave to the lies of the enemy, which kept me from moving forward or growing into who I was created to be.

I was created by the Creator in His likeness to be set apart. To be a daughter of the Most High God. I was created by the Purpose Maker, for His purpose. That His will would be glorified through me. Woe is me, that I would even get the privilege to be in the presence of God, let alone be a partaker of His will. Thank you, Abba, Father, for allowing me to be a living sacrifice, a vessel to be used for your purpose and for your glory to shine through me from the Holy Spirit that dwells within me.

The Blood Defines Me

The world calls me a survivor.

A victim of domestic violence.

A battered woman.

Fragile and broken.

The world tried to silence me.

Labeling me with
all these names.

Trying to hide my true title.

But this world doesn't know me.

My identity comes
from the Trinity.

Need an explanation?
Go read 1 John 3.

I'm not a survivor; I'm a
recipient of salvation.

I'm not a victim, but victorious
by His resurrection.

I'm not a battered woman
but a beloved daughter of
the Most High God.

I'm not fragile or broken,
but freed and renewed.

I'm none of the things
this world calls me.

For these names bring
pity upon one's trials
and testimonies.

Let me introduce you
to the new me.

My names are…

Worthy, loved, cherished,
beautiful, restored,
reborn, enough, whole,
and a child of God!

These names are mine
for eternity.

This is because the blood of
Jesus Christ defines me.

I Don't Walk Alone

Come take this journey with me and see,

This joy that has been living in me.

It will be hard to explain; I won't lie.

I'll give you a visual as I try.

Open your heart and take it all in.

Now open your mind, and let's begin.

I am in a dark valley with dangers on all sides.

The enemy is trying to put thoughts of fear in my mind.

But I laugh, knowing the light I need resides within me.

So, I stand firm and call on thee.

His peace falls upon me and joy eliminates out of me.

For the Lord above has heard my cries,

And awakens the Holy Spirit inside of me to spring alive.

Now I walk with God, Jesus, and the Holy Spirit down this valley.

Facing the dangers that surround me boldly and gladly.

For I know I don't do this in my own ability.

But that's fine with me.

I rather have the power of the Trinity to guide
and protect as I watch the enemy flee...

Abba, You Are My All

You granted me another day.

You provide my daily needs.

In the struggles and trials,
You give me joy.

In the darkness, You are my light.

In my sorrows, Your presence
gives me peace.

When I fall short and need
to repent, Your forgiveness is
instantaneously given to me.

In my weakness, You are my strength.

Abba, You are not just
this thing I follow.

Abba, You are everything
I would ever need.

Abba, I pray my heart will desire You
to be everything I would ever want.

I love You, Abba, because
You first loved me.

I am nothing without You.

But with You, I am everything
You created me to be.

Falling Out of and Into

I fell out of love with how
the world saw me.

I fell out of love with the idea
of a man making me whole.

I fell out of love with
acceptance from people.

I fell out of love with the
numbness alcohol gave me.

I fell out of love with the momentary
satisfaction from cigarettes.

I fell out of love with the idea of my
body bringing me affirmation.

I fell out of love with every
lie Satan told me.

And when I fell out of love with
the world, I fell into darkness.

My knees and hands hit rock bottom.

That rock bottom was my final fall.

That rock bottom that I fell
upon was the Cornerstone.

And there…

I fell into the arms of Jesus, who
was awaiting and welcoming.

I fell into the arms of His grace.

I fell into the arms of His mercy.

I fell into the arms of His forgiveness.

I fell into the arms of His salvation.

I fell into the arms of His
unconditional love.

I fell into the arms of the Holy
Spirit and finally found myself.

I fell out of love with the world and
fell in love with Jesus Christ.

Blessed is She Who is Found in Thee

Blessed is she who is found in Jesus Christ.

She is not satisfied with the
things of this world.

No money, food, or man fills her appetite.

Her diet consists of His words,
prayer, and His voice.

She feasts on His Word and ruminates
on it before digesting it.

She is in constant prayer all
day, without ceasing.

She waits on His voice, like that of a
sheep to its Shepherd, before she moves.

Blessed is the woman who is
found in Jesus Christ.

For she is the branch that feeds off His wine.

She is God's fingerprint; without
Him, she has no identity.

She knows that apart from
Him, she is nothing.

Blessed is she who is in Jesus Christ.

For it's there that she finds true, eternal life.

The Face I Seek

I used to look at many faces.

The faces that abused me.

The faces that hurt me.

The faces that used me.

The faces that broke me.

The faces that hated me.

The faces that betrayed me.

All the faces that looked down on me.

Those faces turned me into a different me.

My face started to reflect a bitter me.

An angry, hurt, grudge-filled,
and revengeful me.

I tried to disguise myself with
drugs, sex, and alcohol.

This was until I couldn't recognize
the face looking back at me.

Then I started to seek the face of Jesus.

Within His face, I found many faces.

The faces of forgiveness,
redemption, and salvation.

The faces of healing, mended, and restored.

The faces of love, joy, peace, and freedom.

My focus shifted from many faces to one face.

The face of Jesus is the only face I want to see.

The face of the Creator looking at His creation.

In the same image, showing three:
Father, Son, and Holy Spirit.

The true image and its image bearer
are the only faces I seek to see.

This is the one face I was created to be.

Love Your Enemies

Who are my enemies?

The murderers, the adulterers,
the rapist, or the racist?

The neighbor to the right
or to the left of me?

The rich or the poor?

The mother who abused me, or
the people who accused me?

The person who cut me off in
traffic or the one who cursed
me out and seemed manic?

My sister or brother in Christ
who offended me, or the preacher
who preaches heresy?

My children who disobey me or
the family who betrayed me?

Wait! Why does my definition
of an "enemy" matter?

Why am I trying to lean on my own
understanding of who I call an "enemy"?

Let me go back to the Red Letters.

But God shows his love for us in that while we were still sinners, Christ died for us. Since, therefore, we have now been justified by his blood, much more shall we be saved by him from the wrath of God. For if while we were enemies we were reconciled to God by the death of his Son, much more, now that we are reconciled, shall we be saved by his life.

Romans 5:8-10

OH, NO…THE ENEMY WAS ONCE ME!

6

MY TESTIMONY

As I started to write this, the word gratitude came to mind. The definition of gratitude from the Oxford Languages is the quality of being thankful and the readiness to show appreciation for and to return kindness. This is just a small drop of how I feel towards the Lord. I do not deserve anything He gifts me. No, that is not a typo; I meant gifts, not gives. The Word of God says:

Do not be deceived, my beloved brothers. Every good gift and every perfect gift is from above, coming down from the Father of lights, with whom there is no variation or shadow due to change. Of his own will he brought us forth by the word of truth, that we should be a kind of firstfruits of his creatures.

James 1:16-18

God took all my ugliness and painted a beautiful picture with the ashes of everything He killed within me. This was only because of the salvation I was gifted through Jesus Christ. The death of my old self and the resurrection of the new creation through Jesus is the only reason why I have these testimonies. I was a mess without Jesus. Now I'm living, breathing, and walking proof of the message He has left me to share: The Good News of the Gospel. There is no such thing as having a testimony if you are not first tested and you go through a mourning season.

Each test the Lord has pulled, carried, pushed, or guided me through was of me dying to the desires of my flesh and/or the desires of my deceitful heart. This sanctification process was hard, trying, and long, but oh, so needed! God was showing me what my will led to and where His will for me would lead me. My will always leads me into bondage and imprisonment. God's will frees me from all the bondage and prisons I placed myself in and keeps me free of new chains. God's will is the only will that sets us free and keeps us free. God's will is the free will we should seek.

Wherever you are on this journey, remember there are many seasons, but two that will always return: the stormy seasons and the seasons in the valleys.

The storms cleanse while you rest in Him, and the valley brings growth while you rest in Him. Both are His works, for His glory. Trust the process, but most importantly, trust in Him. Honestly, when have you seen an ugly valley?

From Bound and Broken to Free and Complete

My life as a sinner had many gifts.

Yes, Satan gives rewards
after each and every sin.

Sex out of wedlock with a
man with a heavy fist.

Three beautiful kids, but seven years of
imprisonment is what the gift gave.

Ran from that situation and
ran into the alcohol bottle.

That bottle gave me courage, freedom
of flesh, and out came Jezebel.

But once she was gone, the gifts of
guilt, shame, and regret came.

So that alcohol bottle is where I
stayed, so Jezebel could play.

Two years bound to that
gift and all its shame.

So, I traded that gift for
a worldly marriage.

One beautiful daughter, mental
and emotional abuse, and
infidelities now unwrapped.

Twelve years was the length
of that gift's stay.

Finally, I went to church and
said *Jesus, have Your way.*

Then He did only what God can do and
started taking those gifts of Satan away.

God became my eternal gift
and started to free me from the
bonds those gifts had made.

He was the key to every lock
for every jail cell and chain.

He freed me from mental health with
the key labeled Great Physician.

He freed me from lust with
the key labeled Forgiven.

He freed me from shame, guilt, and
regret with the key labeled Redeemed.

He freed me from alcoholism with
the key labeled Living Water.

God has broken every chain and opened
every jail cell I placed myself in

Because Jesus is the one
and only Master Key.

He even has the key to free me from me.

When I Saw God's First Miracle

Great Thanksgiving spent in
Brooklyn with the family.

Back at Mami's place on
12th Street and Ave. B.

My cousin ran into my room to tell
me Robert's choking on something.

I ran to see what was happening.

There in front of me was Robert's
little body, shaking, foaming, seizing;
I just dropped to my knees.

My body froze, and then
someone pushed past me.

I couldn't move but heard people calling
911 and trying to get him to breathe.

I finally see cops running out
of the house with him.

I ran behind them outside in the cold.

They were doing CPR on the hood of
their car; Robert looked so alone.

The EMTs are now here working
on him for what feels like years.

Finally, we're on the way to the
hospital, where doctors and nurses
are outside waiting for us to appear.

The wait felt like forever until I heard
CODE BLUE! CODE BLUE!

I felt death laughing in my ear.

I ran into the room and threw
my body on top of him and told
him, *Don't worry, God is near.*

I don't know what happened after
that; I must have been sedated.

Because I woke up in the bed next to
my son, who was highly medicated.

The date was November 2005.

That's when the thought
first crossed my mind.

That Jesus is real and is still alive.

Since the start of my life,
I have had to fight.

But my son's life had barely started, and
he had already almost seen the light.

I Used to Be a Mess

Rolling around and
bathing in sin.

Drinking and smoking, you
know that YOLO way of living.

Waking up and replaying and
repeating this way of life.

Taking the air in my
lungs for granted.

Cursing, fighting, and
just being a fool.

This is what I once
called a good time.

Dancing in all kinds of clubs.

Letting men get a free rub.

Then Jesus said, "Enough!"

I surrendered all of
myself to Him.

I no longer needed a
substance to comfort me.

For Jesus is my sustainer
who validates me.

Jesus turned my mess
into a message.

Now clothed in His blood
of righteousness.

Forgiven of all my sins
because His grace and
mercies always win.

YOLO turned into
giving Jesus control.

Praising Him daily for all
He has saved me from.

Jesus took me from hell
and seated me at His
table for all eternity.

I Am Seen

Ejected by the womb that held
me out of obligations.

Raised by many, some who loved
me and some who resented me.

From house to house, shelter
to shelter, rinse and repeat.

Finally, some stability, what a birthday
wish come true, or so I thought.

Here's where my life gets rough.

Mom meets man, man moves
in, and man beats kids; as the
oldest, I must step in.

Perfect student, perfect kid, I had
to be, so I wouldn't be beaten.

Because I had to be strong
for what was coming.

Every time a belt was raised,
I ran and took my place.

A shield I became for my
siblings every day.

Full of marks and burns,
I finally ran away.

To the woman who insisted
my life be saved.

Cops, paramedics, and finally
my dad's on the scene.

With tears in his eyes and words
of apology out of his mouth.

I felt safe in their pain and their sorrow.

Here I am at the age of eight,
full of hate and full of shame.

Full custody was granted to my dad,
but the excitement didn't last long.

Under his care came the
molestation and rape by those he
trusted, as he worked late.

Eighty-nine different pills taken
for the pain, the first attempt at
suicide, guess what, I failed.

Forced back to the woman whose
womb never wanted me.

This was for my safety; man, the irony.

Rebellion kicked in, and here
comes the teen pregnancies.

I was stuck with a twenty-one-
year-old man; I was just sixteen.

Three beautiful kids and seven
years of domestic battery.

I drank a bottle of Prodoxid,
2nd attempt at suicide, and
guess what? I failed again.

> Hello, is this safe horizon?
> Please, come help me.

Another shelter here, enters the alcohol,
and boom, alcoholism becomes me.

Oh, yes, and my second kid was
diagnosed with an incurable disease.

> My life sucks, and I'm
> only twenty-one.

Got a place of my own, going to school,
finally things are turning around.

Married for the money, sex, drugs, and
alcohol, and yes, the bottle is still in play.

Infidelity, insecurities, arguments,
mental, emotional, and verbal abuse.

Well, it's the best I'll get; I'll just
drink some more anyway.

Alcohol poisoning, vomiting in my
sleep, and a third attempt at suicide.
Can't I get anything right?

Road to sobriety, and now my
son needs brain surgery.

The night before the operation,
I found a Gideon's Bible. You
got to be kidding me.

I pick it up mockingly and say,
What do you have for me?

This Jesus my grandmother serves,
the God she so loves, this man that
died for some, but forgot this one.

The Bible flips open to Psalm 23.

I read in anger, in pain, and end
in tears, and start to pray.

Not for me, but for my son.

This is the day my heart started
to change from stone to flesh.

This Jesus I was introduced to as a babe.

Finally met me as an adult
in my lowly place.

Three years later, I was saved.

Psalm 22:23-24 says, *You who fear the
Lord, praise him! All you offspring of Jacob,
glorify him, and stand in awe of him,
all you offspring of Israel! For he has not
despised or abhorred the affliction of the
afflicted, and he has not hidden his face from
him, but has heard, when he cried to him.*

God heard my cries, He felt my
pain, and He was victorious in
my failed attempts at suicide.

His hands were upon me
every moment of my life.

But He couldn't acknowledge me until
I received the blood of His Son.

For He can only be in the presence
of perfection and Holiness,
because it's who He is.

Now He looks at me, because
He sees these things.

He sees the blood of His Son
Jesus on me and the Holy
Spirit that dwells within.

He sees perfection; He sees
Himself reflecting back at Him.

He sees the Trinity, not me.

This is only the testimony
of my salvation.

This ten-year sanctification brings
its own stories and testimonies.

Abuse

Hey, abuse, where have you been?

Come sit, let's reminisce.

Remember when we first met?

I was confused when you didn't feed me.

But then I got used to the
neglect and beating.

The second time was a little harsher.

You stuck around, and
the hurt was worse.

You stole my innocence
as if it were yours.

I would have preferred the physical
form of you. Or so I thought.

That third time felt like a lifetime.

You came to me in every form.

Your physical abuse was hideous.

Your mental abuse was uglier.

But I wasn't ready for your
verbal and emotional side.

You came to destroy me and almost won.

Three times I tried to end it all
and be freed of your presence.

But three times I failed and felt worse.

I couldn't even do that right.

But anyway, I must go.

Thanks; this talk was therapeutic.

No, you can't come; I've been
freed, and you're not welcome.

Remember when I said I had
failed those three times?

My failures were Jesus's victories.

Every time you came around,
He placed His armor on me.

His strength, love, peace, grace,
and mercies poured out upon me.

He did this even though I had
turned my back on Him.

My choices never included Him.

But He gave His blood and His
life in exchange for mine.

So, I no longer follow you
or fall for your lies.

I follow the One who gave me life.
My Lord and Savior… Jesus Christ.

My Thorn in My Side

Mental health is something
that used to consume me.

My thoughts would overpower me,
deceive me, and try to defeat me.

I have caved into its madness and
believed it lies three times before.

Took pills to quiet the lies that first time.

Drank a bottle of peroxide the
second time it entered my mind.

Finally, I had had enough and ran to
the bottle to end it all the third time.

Three times I failed, and now
I sit here to tell the tale.

God created me with a purpose, and I
won't leave this earth until it's done.

I would be lying if I said I don't
struggle with my mind anymore.

It's January 29, 2024, and I'm
currently struggling with depression;
yes, it's a spiritual war.

But I thank Jesus for allowing
me to struggle with it.

For His name's sake, I no
longer suffer underneath it.

Not only am I free to fight against
this with the armor God gave me.

He also sent me a spiritual
family to walk alongside me.

It may still have an effect on
my energy and emotions.

But we are called to take on
God's strength and not lean on
our own understanding.

My appetite might be non-existent,
but I should not eat bread only.

My sustainability comes from
His living, breathing Word.

I may bend, but with the
Lord, I will never break.

I still go through all these things,
but I no longer face them alone.

From Death to Life

I used to walk in sin, now walking in your peace.

I was told my life was over because I became a teen mom.

You told me you blessed me with them to save me.

I used to feel like I was wearing a scarlet letter.

Now I'm clothed in garments of salvation.

I came to you wearing filthy rags.

You dressed me in a robe of your righteousness.

I was shattered and broken.

You restored me and made me whole.

I felt forsaken and alone.

You gave me forgiveness and called me friend.

I was walking this earth while dead (call me a walker).

You died on a cross, rose again, and salvation is now born.

So, I will die to myself daily to receive the life you gave me.

Lord, here I am, a living sacrifice; Lord, have Your way.

I am no longer dead and in that grave where my sins now lie.

You exchanged Your life for mine.

Thank You, my Lord and Savior, Jesus Christ.

Against My Will

I remember how lost, confused,
and scared I was.

I needed to tell someone,
but who could I trust?

I went to him and told him
what was happening.

He had no reaction and just said,
"Okay, so tell somebody."

His cold emotion gave me no
comfort, so I told nobody.

Months passed, and he
started to fondle me.

He was my age, and it was already
happening, so I let it be.

We did things we knew were wrong,
like kissing and touching each other.

I honestly did it out of fear, and now I
have more wounds and unseen scars.

He would threaten to tell on me and
expose this deep secret I kept.

I started smoking pot at the age of
thirteen just to become numb from it all.

Man, I hated him, and every chance I
got, I started a fight so we could brawl.

After a while, I got tired of the secret
and came forward with the molestation.

The man was forced to move out
because of this information.

But the damage was done,
and it took me until the next
school year for a fresh start.

Now in eighth grade, no more smoking,
and a contestant in the school pageant.

Life was a lot better, and
I felt so much safer.

I remember the night it happened and
I still struggle with those memories.

I decided to get high and drunk
with some "friends" that day.

I didn't get home until after my "pageant
rehearsal" that never actually took place.

I lied to my strict dad to have my way.

I just didn't know my deceit
towards my dad would come back
and cause me the pain it did.

I was so out of it; I got home and
lied and said I was exhausted.

The truth was, I was so intoxicated
that my head was spinning
and mentally distorted.

I went straight to my room and turned
off the light, and went to bed.

I felt something touch me softly
and tried to open my eyes.

I felt a kiss and thought I was
dreaming; wait, this isn't right.

Finally able to open my eyes, it took me
a few seconds to adjust my eyesight.

I was in disbelief seeing him on top of
me, but I still couldn't move normally.

I tried to push him off, but
wasn't strong enough.

He told me to be quiet and was
gentle, but I just felt the disgust.

I kept saying no, but he just kept
going, and my voice was hushed.

Once he was done, he lay down and
went to sleep; I lay there stunned.

This was my fault for
drinking and smoking.

I just lay there knowing and accepting
I would always be broken.

Man, I hate this room!

I kept my silence for two weeks,
acting as if everything was fine.

I slipped up and told my three best
friends, one who went and reported it.

Next thing I know, I'm at a precinct and
being interrogated and accused of lying.

I told my story, and the officer said,
"I don't believe you because you are
way fatter and bigger than him."

I closed my mouth after that,
knowing they had already closed
the case before I even walked in.

I was sent back to the mother who
never wanted me, so I rebelled
and found a man to "love" me.

All I did was run from one form of
abuse to another, and BOOM!

I became a teenage mom instantly.

I didn't go to that side of
my "family" for years.

They never believed me, and they
moved on with life; I just disappeared.

When I finally went back, I was an
alcoholic and had no cares in the world.

I didn't care if they didn't
want me around.

I was there for the partying
and drinking.

Their feelings were none of my concern.

This went on for a while, and before I
moved to Florida, I visited one last time.

I walked into that house and knew it
was the day I would say farewell.

It would be my final goodbye,
but I didn't know why.

God had taken away my
bitterness and evil thoughts I
had for everyone involved.

God healed me, and I was unaware of it.

Until I stepped back into the
place that broke me.

God gave me peace and allowed
me to forgive them; He released
me from that imprisonment.

I wouldn't change anything that
happened; may God get the Glory.

Waiting on the Lord

The definition of waiting is staying
where one is or delaying action
until a particular time or until
something else happens.

The Bible says:

*The Lord is good to those who wait
for him, to the soul who seeks him.*

Lamentations 3:25

Do not be anxious about anything, but in everything by prayer and supplication with thanksgiving let your requests be made known to God. And the peace of God, which surpasses all understanding, will guard your hearts and your minds in Christ Jesus.

Philippians 4:6-7

*Trust in the Lord with all your heart, and
do not lean on your own understanding.
In all your ways acknowledge him, and
he will make straight your paths.*

Proverbs 3:5-6

I didn't know what this really
meant until the Lord placed
me in the valley of waiting.

So come, follow me.

Into this thing I call the waiting season.

I lost my apartment, now I'm
forced to live with my sister.

Three adults, eleven children, two
bedrooms, where's the liquor?

No, God, please forgive me;
this isn't the answer.

It's a daily struggle to be the peace
in a place full of sinful cancer.

I finally decided to remove myself and
my children from that situation.

I stop and stare at this red hotel door,
room 136, our new living location.

I opened the door and prayed to God,
Lord, have Your way; I fully trust in You.

There is no kitchen, two queen-
sized beds, and one mini fridge;
man, this can't be true.

I sat in the tub crying for hours
while God was reminding me
that things would get better.

I climbed out of that tub, weak
and tired, but my spirit had this
newfound peace for this endeavor.

Lord, here I am, whatever
I must do, I will obey.

Now, Lord, please keep Your
promises to me, and may Your
Holy Spirit be on display.

The monthly hotel stay was $3,600.00.

Sixteen-eighteen hours of door dashing
and barely seeing my children, but
every thirty days, I was able to pay.

While dashing, I let the Bible
play instead of music.

I was learning the Word and
how to praise and worship God;
man, it was therapeutic.

In that car, I healed, and in that hotel, I
met the peace of God like never before.

I was still attending church and
began to get more involved,
growing in my thirst for God.

My faith got stronger, and I started
to change from the inside out.

My love and reverence for the
Lord grew, and my worship went
from a whisper to a shout.

I submitted to the will of
God while I waited.

I became more obedient to
His voice as I waited.

I found my identity in Jesus
Christ, but I was still waiting.

I experienced His joy.

My community got bigger.

My situation no longer mattered.

My church became family.

My children found their
own community.

My knowledge of God grew deeper.

Oh, hold on, did I mention
I was still waiting?

God became my first love.

My Provider.

My Comforter.

My Redeemer.

My Shelter.

My Safe Place.

God became my everything, but most
importantly, He became enough.

So here I am, almost two
years later, still waiting.

Now that I can see the deliverance
from the hotel, it saddens me.

I cry out, Lord, if Your peace departs
from me, I don't want to leave.

For I choose You, Jesus, in
this small place, full of Your
peace, mercy, and grace.

Over a bigger home that will
provide more space, but Your
presence has no trace.

In His mercy and in His love, He
knows my heart and why it breaks.

For the peace has started to lift because
something else has started to awaken.

All these blessings I received
in the waiting season.

At His feet and on my face,
His unconditional love poured
out upon this heathen.

Here to encourage you in your wait.

The end of it will be on
time and never late.

And I am sure of this, that he who began a good work in you will bring it to completion at the day of Jesus Christ.

Philippians 1:6

7

PRAYERS

Prayer is the core of Christianity. Prayer is the direct line to communication with Abba, Father. Without it, we do not have power or access to the heavenly places. The price to gain this access was the death of Jesus Christ! What other way to stress the importance of prayers than pointing you back to what God says about praying.

If any of you lacks wisdom, let him ask God, who gives generously to all without reproach, and it will be given him. But let him ask in faith, with no doubting, for the one who doubts is like a wave of the sea that is driven and tossed by the wind.

James 1:5-6

And the prayer of faith will save the one who is sick, and the Lord will raise him up. And if he has committed sins, he will be forgiven.

James 5:15

And he came out and went, as was his custom, to the Mount of Olives, and the disciples followed him. And when he came to the place, he said to them, "Pray that you may not enter into temptation." And he withdrew from them about a stone's throw, and knelt down and prayed, saying, "Father, if you are willing, remove this cup from me. Nevertheless, not my will, but yours, be done." And there appeared to him an angel from heaven, strengthening him. And being in agony he prayed more earnestly; and his sweat became like great drops of blood falling down to the ground. And when he rose from prayer, he came to the disciples and found them sleeping for sorrow, and he said to them, "Why are you sleeping? Rise and pray that you may not enter into temptation."

Luke 22:39-46

Praying at all times in the Spirit, with all prayer and supplication. To that end, keep alert with all perseverance, making supplication for all the saints, and also for me, that words may be given to me in opening my mouth boldly to proclaim the mystery of the gospel.

Ephesians 6:18-19

These are just some of my favorite scriptures on prayer and the place from which prayer gets its power. I looked this up on Google, so show me some grace. The King James Version of the Bible mentions the words prayer, petition, supplication, and beseech about 693 times. Prayer is a necessity.

With that being said, let us pray…

Prayer

Prayer – give God all the
glory and thanksgiving.

Repent – turn from your sin
and ask for forgiveness.

Atone – be ready to pay for the
consequences of your sins.

Yield – surrender yourself
as a living sacrifice.

Extricate – let go of all that
isn't of God and be set free.

Receive – let God give you all your
daily possessions and needs.

Being in prayer gives you all the
equipment and powers up the armor
you need to put on each day.

Prayer For Healing

Abba Father,

I come to you in the name of Your Son, Jesus, and not my own. For He is the reason I could approach Your throne. For He has left His Holy Spirit to dwell in us. Hallelujah, thank You, Jesus. I humbly come to You carrying a burden alongside ____________________. Lord, You know and feel their physical pain, so we are coming to You, the Healer above all healers, the one who created us and knows us in our inmost being. We are praying for supernatural, powerful healing from the spiritual heavenly place, in the name of Jesus! Lord, what better way to come to You with all prayers, thanksgiving, and supplication, than with Your living, breathing Word.

Bless the Lord, O my soul, and all that is within me, bless his holy name! Bless the Lord, O my soul, and forget not all his benefits, who forgives all your iniquity, who heals all your diseases, who redeems your life from the pit, who crowns you with steadfast love and mercy, who satisfies you with good so that your youth is renewed like the eagle's.

Psalm 103:1-5

Be gracious to me, O Lord, for I am languishing; heal me, O Lord, for my bones are troubled.

Psalm 6:2

The Lord sustains him on his sickbed; in his illness you restore him to full health.

Psalm 41:3

Lord, we are thankful for Your Word. We know that we can come boldly before You, asking for healing, wellness, and restoration of the spirit and body.

Gracious words are like a honeycomb, sweetness to the soul and health to the body.

Proverbs 16:24

So, Jesus, in Your name, have mercy on ______________ and receive these words and my plea for their health, like that of sweet honeycomb. I declare Your healing over their life, in Your mighty name, Jesus! Your power is beyond measure, so powerful that Your healing power can fall on______________________, this very second, without me even having to lay hands on them! So, I declare and claim your healing on ______________________ right now, in Your mighty, powerful, and merciful name Jesus Christ! AMEN!

Birthday Prayer

Abba, Father,

On this special day, You created _________________ but had them in Your heart before You laid the foundations of this world. You saw ______________ as Your child before You placed them in their mother's womb. You called _____________ into the body of Christ, before their physical body was even formed. Abba, I give You thanks for _______________. They are a blessing to all who come to know them because they first came to know You, Jesus. They love others because of the new heart you gave them.

Abba, I celebrate and acknowledge You today. Today is the day You ordained for _______________ to be a living, breathing, wonderfully made creation of Yours. Thank You, Abba, for this blessing in our lives. I ask for Your protection and guidance over _______________. Shield them from harm. Surround them with Your angels and continue to lead them along the path of Your righteousness. May _________________ always walk in the light of Your love.

I thank you, in advance, Jesus, for the laughter and joy that they bring into my life. I pray that You continue to bless _________________ with a joyful spirit, a contagious smile, and a heart that overflows with Your love.

I pray for their mental and emotional well-being. In a world filled with challenges, give ______________ Your resilience, peace of mind, and a heart full of gratitude. May they find strength in times of adversity and always see Your birth, sacrifice, and resurrection in their lives.

I pray for blessings over every relationship in their lives. Whether it's marriage, family bonds, or friendships. May they be surrounded by love, understanding, and support from those around them.

Above all else, I pray the blood of Jesus Christ over them. That everything they do is Christ-centered. Thank You for allowing me to be a part of their lives. May we be encouraged, sanctified, corrected, and held accountable by the conviction of Your Holy Spirit that dwells within us. In Jesus's name, I pray this blessing of prayer over the lives of my blood-bought family member ______________ in Christ Jesus.

In Jesus's name, I lift this prayer to You, Abba.

Amen.

Prayer for Refilling of the Holy Spirit

Abba, Father,

I come into Your presence in the name of Your mighty Son, Jesus Christ. Lord, I lay ________________ at Your feet. You alone know the path You have placed them on, but it doesn't mean this path hasn't emptied their cup. Lord, You led me to these scriptures.

Even though I walk through the valley of the shadow of death, I will fear no evil, for you are with me; your rod and your staff, they comfort me. You prepare a table before me in the presence of my enemies; you anoint my head with oil; my cup overflows. Surely goodness and mercy shall follow me all the days of my life, and I shall dwell in the house of the Lord forever.

Psalm 23:4-6

Summon your power, O God, the power, O God, by which you have worked for us...O kingdoms of the earth, sing to God; sing praises to the Lord, [Selah] to him who rides in the heavens, the ancient heavens; behold, he sends out his voice, his mighty voice. Ascribe power to God, whose majesty is over Israel, and whose power is in the skies. Awesome is God from his sanctuary; the God of Israel—he is the one who gives power and strength to his people. Blessed be God!

Psalm 68:28, 32-35

As a reminder that we find our strength, rest, and fulfillment in You, Father, please fill ______________'s spiritual cup. Give them the portion they need and their daily bread for Your will to be done. Place Your Armor over __________________ and keep Your promise to them.

Though they plan evil against you, though they devise mischief, they will not succeed. For you will put them to flight; you will aim at their faces with your bows. Be exalted, O Lord, in your strength! We will sing and praise your power.

Psalm 21:11-13

Lord, may You refill, refresh, restore, and replenish ________________'s Holy Spirit that dwells within them. May You pour out Your strength, endurance, sustainability, mercy, grace, unconditional love, favor, and all that You are upon them. Carry them through this walk as they hold fast to You and Your living, breathing Word. We love You, Abba. Forever and ever. For You alone are HOLY! HOLY! HOLY!

In Jesus's name, I declare a full cup of Your healing and restoration of Your Holy Spirit on ____________. Amen!

The Battle is Already Won

Abba, Father, may we be reminded of the things already said to the disciples.

Jesus answered them, "Do you now believe? Behold, the hour is coming, indeed it has come, when you will be scattered, each to his own home, and will leave me alone. Yet I am not alone, for the Father is with me. I have said these things to you, that in me you may have peace. In the world you will have tribulation. But take heart; I have overcome the world."

John 16:31-33

But thanks be to God, who gives us the victory through our Lord Jesus Christ. For God gave us a spirit not of fear but of power and love and self-control. Lord, the power of Your Spirit has been around since the beginning. Your Word tells us who fights our battles, even in the Old Testament.

And he said, "Listen, all Judah and inhabitants of Jerusalem and King Jehoshaphat: Thus says the Lord to you, 'Do not be afraid and do not be dismayed at this great horde, for the battle is not yours but God's.'"

2 Chronicles 20:15

Lord, for the battles are Yours, and You have been and will always be victorious in them all. May we continue to suit ourselves with Your armor, and we stand firm on the strong foundation You have built as the cornerstone. May we give You all the honor, praise, and glory forever and ever.

Hallelujah! The battles are already won by the power and the blood of Jesus Christ, our Lord and Savior.

In Jesus's name I pray! Amen! Amen! Amen!

Prayer for the Armor of God

Thank You, Abba Father, for Your unconditional love. A love so incomprehensible, all-consuming, and undeserving. A love so powerful that You sent Your one and only Son to atone for us. This love is shown in the book of John.

"For God so loved the world, that he gave his only Son, that whoever believes in him should not perish but have eternal life."

John 3:16

What a gift You have lavished upon us. Jesus, thank You for Your obedience, trust, and love towards our Heavenly Father. We are grateful that You would come and be the perfect sacrificial lamb and complete atonement for our sins, not only for us, but to fulfill the perfect will of our Abba, Father. Who are we that we not only receive this free gift, but we have the privilege to read about the love between God, the Father, and His Son, Jesus, again, in the book of John.

"For I have come down from heaven, not to do my own will but the will of him who sent me. And this is the will of him who sent me, that I should lose nothing of all that he has given me, but raise it up on the last day."

John 6:38-39

Jesus, because of You, we now have an inheritance in Your kingdom.

The inheritance is spoken about in the book of Ephesians.

In him we have obtained an inheritance, having been predestined according to the purpose of him who works all things according to the counsel of his will, so that we who were the first to hope in Christ might be to the praise of his glory.

Ephesians 1:11-12

Abba, thank You for choosing us to be recipients of this inheritance. Jesus, You are enough, Your blood is enough. If that was all You gave, it would have been enough. You not only saved us, but You have also adopted us into your family. You made sure we would be protected on this earth, every day, until You returned. Before you ascended into Heaven, You left us with two extra things. These things would keep us protected against the spiritual battles You knew we would encounter. Jesus, thank You for Your Holy Spirit.

Jesus said to them again, "Peace be with you. As the Father has sent me, even so I am sending you." And when he had said this, he breathed on them and said to them, "Receive the Holy Spirit."

John 20:21-22

Jesus, You give nothing but life! You breathed Your life into us by the Holy Spirit. God, it is the same life You gave Adam.

Then the Lord God formed the man of dust from the ground and breathed into his nostrils the breath of life, and the man became a living creature.

Genesis 2:7

Hallelujah!!! Thank You, Abba.

Along with the Holy Spirit, You gave us Your Armor, Lord.

Finally, be strong in the Lord and in the strength of his might. Put on the whole armor of God, that you may be able to stand against the schemes of the devil. For we do not wrestle against flesh and blood, but against the rulers, against the authorities, against the cosmic powers over this present darkness, against the spiritual forces of evil in the heavenly places. Therefore take up the whole armor of God, that you may be able to withstand in the evil day, and having done all, to stand firm. Stand therefore, having fastened on the belt of truth, and having put on the breastplate of righteousness, and, as shoes for your feet, having put on the readiness given by the gospel of peace. In all circumstances take up the shield of faith, with which you can extinguish all the flaming darts of the evil one; and take the helmet of salvation, and the sword of the Spirit, which is the word of God, praying at all times in the Spirit, with all prayer and supplication. To that end, keep alert with all perseverance, making supplication for all the saints.

Ephesians 6:10-18

Lord, may we wake up every morning remembering to place Your armor upon us.

May we place the helmet of salvation over our heads to protect us from the lies of the enemy and to take every thought captive.

For though we walk in the flesh, we are not waging war according to the flesh. For the weapons of our warfare are not of the flesh but have divine power to destroy strongholds. We destroy arguments and every lofty opinion raised against the knowledge of God, and take every thought captive to obey Christ, being ready to punish every disobedience, when your obedience is complete.

2 Corinthians 10:3-6

May we place the breastplate of righteousness over our torso to protect our organs, but above all else, our heart.

Keep your heart with all vigilance, for from it flow the springs of life.

Proverbs 4:23

May we place the belt of truth fastened around us, holding all the garments together, knowing that Your truths are the only way to eternal life.

Jesus said to him, "I am the way, and the truth, and the life. No one comes to the Father except through me."

John 14:6

May we hold up the shield of faith to protect us from the flaming darts of the evil one and all his other attacks.

"No weapon that is fashioned against you shall succeed, and you shall refute every tongue that rises against you in judgment. This is the heritage of the servants of the Lord and their vindication from me, declares the Lord."

Isaiah 54:17

May we lift up the sword of Your Word that will bring life and not death upon others.

For the word of God is living and active, sharper than any two-edged sword, piercing to the division of soul and of spirit, of joints and of marrow, and discerning the thoughts and intentions of the heart. And no creature is hidden from his sight, but all are naked and exposed to the eyes of him to whom we must give account.

Hebrews 4:12-13

"It is the Spirit who gives life; the flesh is no help at all. The words that I have spoken to you are spirit and life."

John 6:63

Finally, may we be ready to walk into this battle with the shoes of peace You have placed on our feet, which is the Holy Spirit.

"But the Helper, the Holy Spirit, whom the Father will send in my name, he will teach you all things and bring to your remembrance all that I have said to you. Peace I leave with you; my peace I give to you. Not as the world gives do I give to you. Let not your hearts be troubled, neither let them be afraid."

John 14:26-27

With all prayers, supplications, and thanksgivings, this armor is activated and ready for today's battles. I pray we yoke ourselves with You, knowing we stand on the firm foundation, built of Your blood poured out for us, for the will of God the Father.

WE STAND IN VICTORY! THANK YOU, ABBA FATHER, THANK YOU, JESUS THE SON, AND THANK YOU, HOLY SPIRIT! DEATH WAS DEFEATED BY THE POWER OF THE TRINITY! AMEN!

Prayer of Intercession for a Christ-Centered Marriage

Abba, Father,

I come to You in reverence and humbly lay myself at Your feet. I come in the name of Your Son, Jesus Christ, and not on my own, in prayer of intercession for Your church body, for those who are under Your covenant of marriage. Lord, please place Your hedge of protection over every marriage that You have joined together. Your Word states:

"But from the beginning of creation, 'God made them male and female.' 'Therefore a man shall leave his father and mother and hold fast to his wife, and the two shall become one flesh.' So they are no longer two but one flesh."

Mark 10:6-8

Your promise follows in:

"What therefore God has joined together, let not man separate."

Mark 10:9

May they cling to these promises and commands. Abba renew a willing spirit. Help them not to point fingers or respond defensively. Teach them how to listen to one another and to incline their ears to listen with their spiritual ears and hear from you. Lord, may they recognize their actions, attitudes, and feelings towards each other. May You constantly remind them to reflect on these things to see each other as Your children. May their words bring life to each other and not death. I ask You to show them, with spiritual eyes, what they need to do to make these things right between them. I pray they continue to seek You individually and as a union. I ask You to work within each of their hearts.

Lord, You promised to guide them in the way they should go. You are a wise Counselor, and You know exactly what they need. I pray that all their hopes and expectations are in You. If outside Christian counseling is necessary, please lead them to the correct one. I trust that You are the answer, Lord. I believe and declare that You will restore, refresh, replenish, and reignite the heart for You they once had. I ask that You breathe new life, new wisdom, and new understanding into each marriage You have joined together.

In the name of Jesus Christ.

Amen!

Prayer For Healing Over Panic and Anxiety

Abba Father,

In the name of Jesus, I come to You with a burden I am so privileged to help carry. A burden that You so graciously bestowed upon all of us, the power to pray against all things, such as panic and anxiety. Praise You, Abba, that we don't have to carry it far. Here I am, Lord. Laying it at the cross, at your feet. Abba, Father, Jesus, Son, and Holy Spirit. I am calling on the divinity of the Trinity. I am declaring your full, miraculous, powerful, healing over ____________________'s whole body! May the blood of Jesus run down on ____________________ from the top of their head to the soles of their feet! Remind ____________________ of Your power and Your grace. Fill ____________________ with Your peace. We cannot beat this on our own, but we have You, Lord, and You have already paid the ultimate price to carry all our burdens. Calm ____________________ with Your quiet words of love, forgiveness, mercy, and grace. Through Your sacrifice, You have set ____________________ free of all things of this world.

"I have said these things to you, that in me you may have peace. In the world you will have tribulation. But take heart; I have overcome the world."

John 16:33

Though if I should wish to boast, I would not be a fool, for I would be speaking the truth; but I refrain from it, so that no one may think more of me than he sees in me or hears from me. So, to keep me from becoming conceited because of the surpassing greatness of the revelations, a thorn was given me in the flesh, a messenger of Satan to harass me, to keep me from becoming conceited. Three times I pleaded with the Lord about this, that it should leave me. But he said to me, "My grace is sufficient for you, for my power is made perfect in weakness." Therefore I will boast all the more gladly of my weaknesses, so that the power of Christ may rest upon me. For the sake of Christ, then, I am content with weaknesses, insults, hardships, persecutions, and calamities. For when I am weak, then I am strong.

2 Corinthians 12:6-10

May You gift _________________ with the endurance and strength to struggle with this thorn in their side for Your purpose, for Your glory, and for Your name's sake! For it is because of the power of the blood of Jesus Christ that they no longer suffer under it.

Free _________________'s mind, thoughts, heart, and anything that isn't of You and replace them with Your peace and place your armor over them. Thank You for listening to our prayers. We know it's already fixed! Thank You, Jesus, for Your power that still saves, heals, restores, and makes one whole again. In the mind, body, and spirit! Hallelujah!! In the name of Jesus, the King above all kings, our Savior, our Redeemer, our God, in Jesus's name! Amen!

A Special Letter to You. The Reader.

To the Hurting, Lost, Sinful, Angry, Lustful, Imprisoned, and Lowly Reader,

Yes, you, are you not tired? I'm not talking about just physical tiredness, but that mental, emotional, and spiritual exhaustion. Are you not tired of living the same way? Are you not tired of having to struggle and beg for your next place to lay your head? Are you not tired of feeling like your life was created for suffering alone? Are you not tired of using your body to make it through life? Are you not tired of the pain and hurt you feel daily, caused by others? Are you not tired of those thoughts that invade your mind? Are you not tired of being angry all day or having a short fuse? Are you not tired of being in that lonely, dark place? Are you not tired of feeling tired from the inside out and not knowing why? I have just the rest you need.

"Come to me, all who labor and are heavy laden, and I will give you rest. Take my yoke upon you, and learn from me, for I am gentle and lowly in heart, and you will find rest for your souls. For my yoke is easy, and my burden is light."

Matthew 11:28-30

These are the words Jesus spoke. He is calling on you to come to Him. He is waiting with open arms to take all your burdens and to relieve you of this weight you have been carrying. For you to be able to have empty hands, to receive

His salvation, forgiveness, mercy, grace, love, kindness, and so much more. You are not too far gone; you are not a lost cause. You were not created by mistake without a purpose. The love Jesus has for His Father is why He came down and died on the cross. He came down from His place of glory because His Father in Heaven willed Him to. God willed this so we could have a relationship with Him. Yes, the blood of Jesus was shed for you, too. But Jesus didn't just die, but the Father raised Him back to life so we would have full access to our Heavenly Father. He is the gap, the bridge we must cross, and the gatekeeper into that connection to the Father forever.

Jesus said to him, "I am the way, and the truth, and the life. No one comes to the Father except through me. If you had known me, you would have known my Father also. From now on you do know him and have seen him."

John 14:6-7

If you are questioning, "How can I receive such a thing?" Here is your answer:

Because, if you confess with your mouth that Jesus is Lord and believe in your heart that God raised him from the dead, you will be saved. For with the heart one believes and is justified, and with the mouth one confesses and is saved. For the Scripture says, "Everyone who believes in him will not be put to shame."

Romans 10:9-11

If we confess our sins, he is faithful and just to forgive us our sins and to cleanse us from all unrighteousness.

1 John 1:9

I think I can say with truth that Jesus wants to forgive you and cleanse you of all your sins, guilt, and shame because He loves you! If you believe this calling is for you, just say this prayer:

"Abba, Father, I know I have sinned against You and have been running from You. Lord, I am tired of running, I am tired of this pain, hurt, anger, bitterness, loneliness, darkness, and things I don't understand. Lord, please forgive me of all my sins. I ask that You would pour Your blood over me and cover me with Your righteousness. May Your blood fall on me, from the top of my head to the soles of my feet. May Your blood wash away all my stains and make me white as snow. I ask that You come into my stony heart, crack it wide open, and relieve the heart of flesh You have given me. I pray that You will kill and bury the old me and resurrect me by baptizing me with Your Holy Spirit. Holy Spirit, fall upon me and make my body Your temple. Holy Spirit, I invite You into my heart and ask that You take residence here. May You dwell in me for eternity. Jesus, have Your way in me. Abba, may Your will be done and may my will be silenced. Lord, take all of me away and fill me with all of You. I repent of my sins, in exchange for Your forgiveness, Your grace, Your mercy, and for Your Holy Spirit. In the mighty and powerful name of Your Son, Jesus, I declare this prayer over my life today and forever more.

Amen!"

Congratulations on the death of your flesh and Happy Birthday on your rebirth!!

Therefore, if anyone is in Christ, he is a new creation. The old has passed away; behold, the new has come.

2 Corinthians 5:17

"Just so, I tell you, there will be more joy in heaven over one sinner who repents than over ninety-nine righteous persons who need no repentance."

Luke 15:7

Letters to My Children and Granddaughters

1/30/2024

Dear Nia (Rainia),

I knew your letter would be the first I wrote. Not because you are the oldest, but because your letter would be the hardest one to write. But I didn't know how hard it was until I started to think about what to tell you. So let me start with the obvious. I am sorry that you received the crappiest, most sinful mother than the rest of them. You were forced to grow up too early; you received all my hurt based on the trauma I endured. I placed all my failures upon you and expected you to succeed so I could live vicariously through you. You were supposed to be the only thing I did right in my life. I am sorry for placing all of these high expectations on you. It was a weight too heavy for me to carry, so the only logical thing was to place it on you. Makes sense, right? I was obviously delusional! I was only sixteen years old when I had you. I was a baby myself, trying to raise a baby. We grew up together, which is the sad truth. The "love" I gave you was based on what I knew. You got the abused mother, the broken little girl, the lost and unworthy soul, and the sinner part of me. You've watched me get drunk, you partied with me, you went everywhere with me, you helped me with the other kids, and you have been in every crappy and lowly situation I placed us in. You have had to endure every stupid decision I made and were forced to deal with it, because I am the mother, and you must do what I say. You have watched me pass out, pee on myself, dance very inappropriately, curse, fight, scream, and so much more. You have seen my ugliest parts and still stand here with me today. I "loved" you out of my hurt, pain, grief, anger, grudges, and so much more. I "loved" you high, drunk, unstable, and unfit. Then I got saved.

It broke my heart to know I was the cause of the path you took. Then I had the audacity to get mad at you for taking it. I was such a hypocrite. You went through very similar trials. You didn't feel worthy of someone's love. You went through your own abuse and endured your own domestic violence situation. You also became a teen mom, getting drunk and high as I did. I was watching you become me, and it was the most painful thing to witness. I watched as the cycle repeated itself. You and your siblings are why my prayer life is so strong. Again, I owe you another apology. So, I just kept praying. Even though we had a lot of ups and downs, God still sustained our relationship. We argued, fist-fought, and made up like we were high school friends. I allowed this. I was taught children had nothing to say, they just did as they were told, and there were never any apologies. I was taught to hide my feelings and "don't cry if you didn't want something to cry for." The way I was taught worked for me in the generation I grew up in, but that parenting was for my protection, right? So, when I was being abused, that parenting was so hypocritical, condescending, and very contradictory to me. I was just confused. I am not making any excuses; I just want to try and explain why you got the mother you did. I have watched you go through everything I put you through. By the time I got sober and cleaned up, it was too late. You never stood a chance…

So, I thought. Little did I know that God had a plan for you and me. Through all your struggles, you graduated from high school, you became a mother, you became an Esthetician, but most importantly, you were saved by Jesus. You started to find your voice, you started to share your feelings and opened up to me more; you started to stay quiet and just ignore people; you started to know your worth and kill your flesh; and you started to let go of all the bad habits and strongholds. You started to grow in your faith and started to find your identity in Jesus Christ. You were finally stepping into who Jesus created you to be.

I will end this letter like this. I want you to know that even as that wicked mother, my heart always recognized that you were the gift that God gave me to save my life. You were the reason I started to fathom the thought of staying in this world. I might not have always shown it, but you and your siblings are the only things that were a blessing in all my sinful decisions. This is my proclamation to the world of how much I love you and how proud I am of you. You have broken many cycles that were generationally worldly. You are worthy of love, you are beautiful, you are doing the best you can as a single mother, and you are who Jesus has called you to be. You are a new creation. I am honored to be called your mom, and I have the privilege of watching you grow into the woman I always knew you would be. I get to see you become better than me! A better woman, mother, and follower of Jesus Christ. You got this because you know God's got you. I love you and I'm so proud of you, Nia!

Love your biggest cheerleader,

- Mom

1/30/2024

What's Up, Robert? My Guy, LOL!

Where do I start with you, Robert? Boy, oh boy, did you give me a run for my money and still do. You were always different. You liked to play alone; you didn't cry much as a baby, and I couldn't understand why you did the things you did as a toddler. Like the time you took all the fish out of the fish tank, and I found them on the carpet, jumping around. Or when you gave the fish dishwashing liquid to drink. It wasn't until you were fifteen months old that I found the answer to my question. You were diagnosed with a rare condition called TSC, also known as Tuberous Sclerosis Complex. From being non-verbal, having seizures, to four brain surgeries, one this past year, and given a long life span of about ten years due to this condition, but here you are against all odds. But I would be lying if I said raising you was easy. The tantrums, the anger, the violence, and all the ugliness that came from raising a child who is missing a large portion of his brain were huge challenges for me. Those multiple surgeries left you with the missing connection between the left side of your brain and the right side. Though you grew physically, your brain will always stay between that of a seven to twelve-year-old boy. This, in itself, causes you to be confused. I could never understand the disconnect you must feel towards your own body and mind.

However, this sickness never stopped you from being helpful to others; you are kind to every person you meet, and you will be the first to talk to a stranger or homeless person. The way you look at people is so beautiful and pure. You don't look at the outside, you just see the person. You feel deeply and love passionately. Please never let anything or anyone take the light God has placed inside you. You are a miracle child, so go out into this fallen world and be that miracle God created you to be, so that others would find Christ. Just like you have. I love you, Robert, and I'm proud to have had the privilege and blessing of watching you grow into the man you are today. Even after this world said you wouldn't be a teenager. ALL GLORY AND PRAISE TO OUR GOD ON HIGH!

THANK YOU, JESUS!

Love your number one advocate (after Jesus),

-Mom

2/12/2024

What's Poppin', Ryan?

Your letter is going to be the most convicting. I have always told you, you are me in male form. When I was pregnant with you, I hid my whole pregnancy. Only your father and aunt knew. Everyone found out the day I went into labor. I always tell this story because you made it a point, your whole life, to make sure everyone knew you were around. You have my brain, my wit, my sarcasm, the protector quality, my strong-mindedness, and you are very independent. You have watched me go through so much with the man who raised you, your siblings, and so much more. I watched you grow up way before your time. You picked up the role of the man of the house and my protector. You were the one who walked alongside me through it all. Yes, we bumped heads, but when things went sideways, you were right by my side. It made me proud and broke my heart at the same time. This role wasn't a choice; it was placed on you. However, this role took away your childhood. You have literally thrown yourself in front of fights between me and your siblings to protect me. But I was the one who was supposed to protect you.

Towards the end of last year, you got yourself into some trouble, but you and I both know that was such a blessing in disguise. I have watched you grow in your faith and walk with the Lord because of it. I have seen you step out in faith and go on a mission trip, only to come back with a changed heart. I have had the privilege to watch you go from that confused little boy (whom I created based on my worldly parenting) into this young man who is following Jesus Christ. The thing I'm most proud of, one of many things, is the way you serve and are willing to help everyone, no matter the situation.

Ryan, thank you for helping carry all these burdens and for stepping into what God has called you to. I can't wait to see where the Lord takes you next. As long as you remember to seek first the Kingdom of God and remember that the Lord promises to bless you and keep you, because He is the Peacemaker, you will be just fine. You will be okay because God's got you.

I love you, and I pray the Lord will allow me time on this earth to watch you become a missionary, a godly husband, and a godly father, if God's plan allows. Keep trusting and placing God first, and you, my son, will be a mighty warrior for the Kingdom of our Lord Jesus.

Love you, My Guy,

-Mom

2/12/2024

Hey Royallin (Mommy's baby),

You are so different from your siblings in every way. You were the only pregnancy that I planned. I tried for two years, and it didn't happen, but the minute I gave up, God gave me you. You were raised by a saved mother and were privileged to be raised in church. You are very sensitive. You weren't raised in New York. You have love and compassion that is led by the Holy Spirit; the Holy Spirit that dwells within you is so powerful. You have been clingy your whole life. You have always laid on top of me since the day you were born. The only problem with that is you are almost as big as me, and you be hurting my back, girl!

Your faith in Jesus Christ makes me so proud. You convict me daily, which can get under my skin at times, especially when it's 7:00 am in the morning and we're in the car circle. You always leave me crying and repenting in the car afterward. I have watched you be bullied in school. I have watched you in pain when your father and I got divorced. I've watched you still hurt from the aftermath, but most importantly, I have watched you bring God into every one of these situations. I pray your faith only gets stronger as you get older. Continue to be that light in a dark world. Keep praying for those children in school and keep praying for your dad and his family, like you always do. Your letter will be the shortest because you are only ten and you haven't lived as rough of a life as your siblings.

I will leave you with this: you are beyond beautiful, you are loved, you are not fat, you are worthy of love, and many do love you tremendously. Just because your father and I split up, that doesn't mean you're a mistake. Those are all the lies of the enemy. Fear isn't of God, so please do not live your life in fear. Don't let your dyslexia hold you back. Keep following God, and He will take you to places you never thought possible. Mommy is SO proud of you.

Remember, people will come and go, but Jesus is with you always. He will never leave you. Last year, you lost your first best friend, and you are still grieving this loss, and that is okay. Grieving is an emotion from God, so you take all the time you need, but don't forget to give it to God. This will be one of many.

I love you and I believe in you!

-Mom

1/13/2024

Hi Mima,

Dior, you have shown me a new kind of love. When your mother called me to tell me she was pregnant with you, I already knew. I shared with her that God gave me a dream about you. I honestly thought you were a little boy because of the hair in my dream. When I saw you in that 4D sonogram, it hit me. You were real, and this was really happening; I was really going to be a grandma. But I was too young to be called grandma, and gave myself the name Mima. I fell in love with the title and everything that came with it.

When your mother's water broke, I was so excited, but I couldn't be there due to COVID-19 restrictions. When I saw you, you had me in the palm of your hand. You are such a blessing to this family. You are spunky, sassy, funny, energetic, dramatic, a girly girl, and spoiled. Watching you grow has been a bittersweet thing. I can't believe you are four years old. Even though I missed some of it, you have always been in my prayers and in my mind.

I can't wait to see what the Lord has in store for you. You know so many Christian songs, but your favorite, at this time of your life, is "Gratitude" by Brandon Lake. "Mima, play hallelujah, play hallelujah," that's what you would say.

Dior, remember that no matter what happens in life, no matter who hurts you, who disappoints you, who turns their backs on you, Jesus never will. I pray that you never see the things your mother did. I pray you will be a willing vessel of the Lord, and that through you, many will come to Christ Jesus.

I also pray that you will be a role model for the generations to come. May God break many chains and generational curses through you! You will always have this letter to remind you of the grace and mercy God has given those before you, and to remind you that Mima loves you so much, even when Mima is no longer around.

Love always,

-Mima

4/6/2025

Well, Hello There, Sah'raya,

I am your Mima Diana. We haven't actually met. Your mommy (Rainia) is scheduled to be induced today. Today is a very special day for your Mima. April 6th was my grandma's birthday. She was the woman who raised me and introduced me to Jesus Christ. For the past four years, I have always asked if she was proud of me and if she is watching her answered prayer for me to be saved, as I walk with Jesus Christ. She never got a chance to see me change my life around, and I never got the chance to talk to her about Jesus as a believer. Now, here it is four years later, and you are scheduled to enter the world on her birthday. I cannot wait to meet you and pray over you. Your mommy's middle name is Lenea, after her, and your middle name will be the same after your mommy and in honor of your great-great-grandmother. To be honest, I had already finished writing this book and submitted it to the editing team. I was in the process of going over it and creating the table of contents, and got to the part of the book "Letters To My Children and Granddaughter" and noticed you didn't have one. I had only written one to your sister, Dior. It was like God was showing me that you would be here before this book was published, and you needed to be acknowledged. God's timing is always perfect. It's so fascinating. He would lead me to write this letter to you on the day you are scheduled to make your grand entrance into this world. I love you already, and I promise to do my best to lead you to Jesus Christ, like my Mami did for me. I promise to love you with the love of Jesus

Christ. I'm sure I will disappoint you at some point because no one is perfect, but with the grace, love, and mercy of Jesus Christ that He freely gives us, we have the gift of forgiveness. We are joyfully awaiting your arrival.

Love always,

Your Mima

Letter to Myself

From: The current Diana
To: The younger Diana

This will be my final letter. I left my final letter to the person who needed it the most…myself. I now understand that my life and all its trials, tribulations, and suffering were for God's glory. God allowed Satan to touch me, knowing that I would be a warrior for His kingdom, a daughter He would adopt through the blood of Jesus, a servant for His great commission, and a survivor because He gave me the endurance and strength I would need to get through it all. God knew this because He created me with the knowledge of all the plans Satan had for me and all the people and things Satan would use to try to make all these plans come to pass. It still blows my mind how much power we give Satan and how much fear we allow him to have over us. Let's talk about this logically. We know God is the creator of all things, including Satan and all his minions. We know that Satan has limited power. Yet, we are so quick to choose Satan and all he offers. We don't mind walking blindly with Satan, but we fear walking with God the same way. Here's an example. When I was not saved, I would drink with the goal of getting so messed up and knowing I might do something crazy, but I didn't care. I was going to enjoy myself. So I would go, get so drunk, and meet a man I don't know. I follow him to a place I have never been to. I expose myself and allow him to have his way with me, not knowing what the outcome would be. All because my mind was already set on enjoying myself. Still don't see it? Let me break it down.

Let's look at my mindset: it was to get drunk first. The Word of God warns us about our minds.

Be sober-minded; be watchful. Your adversary the devil prowls around like a roaring lion, seeking someone to devour.

1 Peter 5:8

Because I wasn't sober-minded, my thoughts are now affected. The thought I had after being drunk was to enjoy myself. The keyword was "self." The Word of God also warns of these things. God warns us about our thoughts and ourselves.

For those who live according to the flesh set their minds on the things of the flesh, but those who live according to the Spirit set their minds on the things of the Spirit. For to set the mind on the flesh is death, but to set the mind on the Spirit is life and peace.

Romans 8:5-6

Finally, I wanted to please my "self," which is my flesh. The Word of God has yet another warning for this as well.

But I say, walk by the Spirit, and you will not gratify the desires of the flesh. For the desires of the flesh are against the Spirit, and the desires of the Spirit are against the flesh, for these are opposed to each other, to keep you from doing the things you want to do. But if you are led by the Spirit, you are not under the law. Now the works of the flesh are evident: sexual immorality, impurity, sensuality, idolatry, sorcery, enmity, strife, jealousy, fits of anger, rivalries, dissensions, divisions, envy, drunkenness, orgies, and things like these. I warn you, as I warned you before, that those who do such things will not inherit the kingdom of God.

Galatians 5:16-21

We are willing to walk blindly with Satan, not worried about where he leads us, and the unknown of Satan doesn't scare us. Yet we are so scared of walking in that same blindness with Jesus, but it's a blindness of walking in faith into the unknown. This is because we walk in the flesh, our physical bodies belong to this world, and it wants everything this world has to offer. A world that God has given authority over to Satan. Jesus spoke of Satan in many scriptures as the ruler of this world. I do urge you to go read the Bible for full context.

"Now is the judgment of this world; now will the ruler of this world be cast out."

John 12:31

So, we follow Satan without question. The flesh is of this world and will not go with us, so it has no desire to follow anything else. Once we have received the Holy Spirit, we then start to seek the will of God, and the fight begins. We start to fight our flesh against our Spirit because the flesh only wants the things of this world, and the Spirit wants the things of its world, which is Heaven. This is why we are scared to follow God with that blind faith, because the Spirit is willing, but the flesh is weak. Matthew, Paul, and James all agree that this is the only battle we each fight individually as believers and followers of Jesus Christ. It's the only fight we must be fighting. The fight we fight amongst ourselves and not amongst one another.

" Watch and pray that you may not enter into temptation. The spirit indeed is willing, but the flesh is weak."

Matthew 26:41

For we know that the law is spiritual, but I am of the flesh, sold under sin. For I do not understand my own actions. For I do not do what I want, but I do the very thing I hate.

Romans 7:14-15

What causes quarrels and what causes fights among you? Is it not this, that your passions are at war within you? You desire and do not have, so you murder. You covet and cannot obtain, so you fight and quarrel. You do not have, because you do not ask. You ask and do not receive, because you ask wrongly, to spend it on your passions. You adulterous people! Do you not know that friendship with the world is enmity with God? Therefore whoever wishes to be a friend of the world makes himself an enemy of God. Or do you suppose it is to no purpose that the Scripture says, "He yearns jealously over the spirit that he has made to dwell in us"? But he gives more grace. Therefore it says, "God opposes the proud but gives grace to the humble." Submit yourselves therefore to God. Resist the devil, and he will flee from you. Draw near to God, and he will draw near to you. Cleanse your hands, you sinners, and purify your hearts, you double-minded.

James 4:1-8

Put on the whole armor of God, that you may be able to stand against the schemes of the devil. For we do not wrestle against flesh and blood, but against the rulers, against the authorities, against the cosmic powers over this present darkness, against the spiritual forces of evil in the heavenly places.

Ephesians 6:11-12

How do we receive the Holy Spirit, in order to follow Jesus with that bold, blind faith, you ask? Let's see God's instructions on this.

And Jesus came and said to them, "All authority in heaven and on earth has been given to me. Go therefore and make disciples of all nations, baptizing them in the name of the Father and of the Son and of the Holy Spirit, teaching them to observe all that I have commanded you. And behold, I am with you always, to the end of the age."

Matthew 28:18-20

"Let all the house of Israel therefore know for certain that God has made him both Lord and Christ, this Jesus whom you crucified." Now when they heard this they were cut to the heart, and said to Peter and the rest of the apostles, "Brothers, what shall we do?" And Peter said to them, "Repent and be baptized every one of you in the name of Jesus Christ for the forgiveness of your sins, and you will receive the gift of the Holy Spirit."

Acts 2:36-38

Well, that seems easy enough, right? Repent of your sins and ask God for forgiveness, and turn from your ways, which are the desires of your flesh and all your wants of this world. But the most important part is which god you are turning to. The Holy Spirit only falls on the heart that is crying out to the true, only living God, Jesus Christ.

Since my last letter is to myself, which will be based on forgiveness, but not of my own, BUT GOD's! The worldly definition of forgiveness is the action or process of forgiving or being forgiven. What?! I'm more confused than everyone. That was not very helpful. Let's see if we can get some clarity from the Bible. Here is what God says about forgiveness:

"For if you forgive others their trespasses, your heavenly Father will also forgive you, but if you do not forgive others their trespasses, neither will your Father forgive your trespasses."

Matthew 6:14-15

"Judge not, and you will not be judged; condemn not, and you will not be condemned; forgive, and you will be forgiven."

Luke 6:37

Let all bitterness and wrath and anger and clamor and slander be put away from you, along with all malice. Be kind to one another, tenderhearted, forgiving one another, as God in Christ forgave you.

Ephesians 4:31-32

Bearing with one another and, if one has a complaint against another, forgiving each other; as the Lord has forgiven you, so you also must forgive.

Colossians 3:13

"And whenever you stand praying, forgive, if you have anything against anyone, so that your Father also who is in heaven may forgive you your trespasses."

Mark 11:25

Wait a minute! So, you are telling me forgiveness is the act of me pardoning or willingly putting my anger, malice, hurt, grudge, hate, and pain aside, based on the wrongdoing of someone else? YES! Forgiveness is not for the other person; it is for us. We are to always be image bearers of Jesus Christ, and He also forgave us of all the wrongdoing we did against Him. Ouch, that stung, didn't it? So, go and take some time and reflect on who in your life you have unforgiveness for and forgive them so that our Abba, Father, can forgive you too.

You always said, "I don't care what people think about me." That was a lie then and is still a lie now. You have always cared, and for some reason, now more than ever. Remember when we were younger and being abused? Remember how hard and loud we would pray silently in our mind for anyone to see our physical scars? What about when we were being molested and how we silently prayed for someone to notice how much we were acting out, how we would get into physical fights, and how angry we had become? Or what about the time we were in that domestic violence relationship? Remember us crying and silently praying on the floor for someone to help us, and our voice falling on deaf ears? Oh, let's not forget our quiet cries and prayers for someone to save us from all of the addictions we now have due to our trauma. There were so many times we prayed silently. Like that time, we prayed for years for our worldly marriage to be saved and for our ex-husband to love us and see our worth.

Well, here we are years later, and we are still silently praying for people to see and notice us in our pain, cries for help, and loneliness. God currently has us on a journey that no one believes is from God, so recently we have been praying for our brothers and sisters in Christ to notice the loneliness we are in because of this journey. As we are writing this, we have finally come to understand why we do this. We pray, cry, and yell for help silently because our voice was silenced as a child. We have also come to realize that, though we felt like we were never seen, heard, loved, or cared for, there was one who had always been there for us, one who heard our every cry. One who cried alongside us. One who protected us and saw all we have gone through. The One we prayed to, but never really understood who we were praying to. The One Mami prayed to. The One whom we never wanted to believe in because we couldn't understand why Mami loved this God so much and praised Him like she did. All we experienced was pain, suffering, rejection, abandonment, and so much more. All of it started to make sense when we were saved in 2015, and received salvation through the Gospel. We started to understand that God sent His one and only Son, Jesus Christ, to be our substitute, an exchange, His life for ours, to die on that cross to atone/pay for the penalty for our sins. He was raised from the dead so that those who believed and loved Him would be raised with Him.

Our life has never been the same. We started to heal and started to love ourselves. God started to teach us how to forgive those who have wronged us and how to ask for forgiveness for those we have wronged. No, we have not received apologies from those who hurt us. At first, we were mad that we never received said apologies. Then God gave us this understanding and wisdom that nowhere in His Word did He ever promise that forgiveness would come from man. God said to come to Him with all our burdens, cares, and ask Him for forgiveness and for us to forgive those who have wronged us, so He, God, can forgive us of all the things we have done against Him. So, there you go. The apology we have been waiting for our whole life. Our childhood, teenage years, and young adulthood came from our very own mouths. The only apology we ever needed or that ever mattered was the one our Abba, Father was waiting for us to give Him, the one asking our Abba, Father to forgive us of our sins in disobedience towards Him; this apology is called repentance. We haven't been the same since, PRAISE GOD!

Since we repented in 2015, we have been freed of our addiction to smoking, drinking, sexual immorality, affirmations from others, and pills. We have been single and celibate for three years and are full of joy because of it. We have finally learned to forgive ourself and have fallen in love with ourself because we have fallen in love with the source, meaning, and true definition of love itself, God. Yes, we still face many trials and tribulations in this life, and man, they have been huge ones. Yes, people still judge, persecute, and talk about us, but we no longer entertain them with anger, a wicked tongue, or physical fighting. We now pray for them to be saved and be able to know the love of God, because we now have God's wisdom to understand they are lost, like we once were. We can understand that hurt people hurt other people, and we have to stop expecting the "dead" (unbelievers) to act like the "living" (saved).

Diana, you did it! You finally encountered the Jesus Mami prayed to and loved so much, and now we are saved. We made it out of hell because of it! Our life is full of joy, love, peace, grace, and so much more. We have four beautiful children, a granddaughter, and another grandchild on the way, which I believe is a girl, shhhhhh don't say anything. We graduated from college, and we are provided for by our Abba, Father! God is currently working on our husband, and we will wait patiently for him, because we know what God has for us will always be better than we could have ever imagined. The love God has for us still makes our head spin. Girlllll, He used us to write this book, US! He saved us from us, and because of that, we lived past the age of twenty-one.

I will end this letter by telling my younger self I am so proud of the woman, mother, daughter, sister, and daughter of the Most High God, you have become. You are so loved by the Creator of the universe and the One who truly created you! All other love is a bonus. You are finally free, and your voice is no longer silenced. Be loud and proud of what God has done for you, His work in and through you, and for what He is still doing that you have yet to see.

I LOVE YOU SO MUCH! KEEP GOING. YOU GOT THIS BECAUSE GOD'S GOT IT AND HE HAS YOU!

ALL FOR THE GLORY AND KINGDOM OF OUR ABBA, FATHER!

Acknowledgements

I want to take this time to thank some people who have encouraged me and pushed me into putting this book out into the world.

For God gave us a spirit not of fear but of power and love and self-control.

2 Timothy 1:7

Abba, Father, none of this would have been possible had You not given me this gift of poetry and the suffering that produced it. All good things come from Heaven above. Lord Jesus, had You not died on the cross for all my sins, I would have never received resurrection along with You, which allows me to testify to this Great News. Holy Spirit, had you not been leading me and providing me with the words for this book, it still would have been this cute idea in my mind. So, thank you, Abba, Father, my Lord and Savior Jesus Christ, and Holy Spirit, for allowing me to be the vessel that You used to create this beautiful masterpiece.

To my family: Dad, thank you for raising me to be the strong woman I am today. You have always supported me to this day. I know if I need anything, you will give it to me if you have it. I thank God for you every day, and I see Him working on you.

To my siblings: Eliza, Jazmyne, Benny, Eleni, Austin, and stepbrother, David. Thank you for the support and love you have given me throughout the years. Yes, we had our ups and downs, but that has never stopped me from loving each and every one of you. I pray the Lord would crack open your stony hearts and you would heed His call of salvation over your lives. Love you all!

To my brothers and sisters in Christ at Live Oaks Bible Church: Thank you for all your help and support through all that my family has faced. You all have helped us through homelessness, with food when we didn't have any, making sure we had everything we needed for hurricanes, when I had no gas, no money, no hope, and no way out. You all were there to love me with the love of Christ and point me back to Jesus. Thank you for holding up my arms when I couldn't.

So Joshua did as Moses told him, and fought with Amalek, while Moses, Aaron, and Hur went up to the top of the hill. Whenever Moses held up his hand, Israel prevailed, and whenever he lowered his hand, Amalek prevailed. But Moses' hands grew weary, so they took a stone and put it under him, and he sat on it, while Aaron and Hur held up his hands, one on one side, and the other on the other side. So his hands were steady until the going down of the sun. And Joshua overwhelmed Amalek and his people with the sword.

Exodus 17:10-13

For allowing me to be vulnerable and not feel any judgment. No, we are not a perfect body, but what body is? A church is a place full of broken believers and lost sinners, just trying to follow a Holy God, and we will fall short every time. A church is known for having true believers based on their actions when one member falls. Do we shun or kick them out, or do we show them mercy and grace and give them our hands to help pull them up and point them back to Christ?

Two are better than one, because they have a good reward for their toil. For if they fall, one will lift up his fellow. But woe to him who is alone when he falls and has not another to lift him up! Again, if two lie together, they keep warm, but how can one keep warm alone? And though a man might prevail against one who is alone, two will withstand him—a threefold cord is not quickly broken.

Ecclesiastes 4:9-12

There is no such thing as church hurt! The church is a representation of Jesus Christ. I have never liked the term "church hurt." It wasn't caused by Jesus. The accurate term should be "people hurt." It was caused by other people. So, thank you, Live Oaks Bible Church members and leaders, for doing your best in trying to follow a Holy God, but knowing you are still human.

To the women at Women in the Word Ministry: Which was the first ministry I ever joined. It laid the foundation for me to understand what it means to be in a community and how to contribute to it. It showed me how to be a follower of Jesus by diving deep into the Word of God. I started changing from the inside out because I was being trained up in the way I should.

Train up a child in the way he should go; even when he is old he will not depart from it.

Proverbs 22:6

Special thanks to Joanne Tittle, who was obedient to the call to keep this ministry going.

To my sisters from Citizen: Thank you for allowing me to be the "mama" in the group. You have all been such a joy and pleasure to be around. Watching you all grow in your faith has been just an honor. I have watched most of you get engaged, married, have children, and so on. It has given me so much hope for my own children. I love you all so very much.

Last, but definitely not least, I would like to just thank some of my friends who have helped me through one or more of the situations in this book. From my elementary to junior high school friends, to the women I met in the shelters, and the women who were just neighbors who watched a lot of my abuse. Thank you all for the support I needed in those times. Your friendship was one of the things that allowed me to keep going and never give up. So, thank you, Rosa, Kennedra, Chasity, Jennifer, Lilly, Jonnie, Ebony, Vennesa, and Desiree.

About The Author

Diana Marie Rosado is a thirty-nine-year-old Hispanic woman from the Lower East Side in Manhattan, New York. She moved a lot and lived with several people, but was mostly raised by her maternal grandparents (Mami and Papi) and her father. Even though she bounced around a lot, the only place that she felt safe was at her grandmother Mami's house on 12th Street and Ave B. That will always be home. She later moved to Brooklyn, New York, and raised her four children, Rainia, Robert, Ryan, and Royallin, in the Bronx. She graduated from college and has her associate's degree in Criminal Justice.

She currently lives in Florida and is engaged to the love of her life, Miguel. She is also a Mima (grandmother) to two beautiful baby girls, Dior, and awaiting the arrival of her second granddaughter, Sah'raya. She is doing her best to follow Jesus Christ and reflect His glory in all that she does. As you read this book, you will see that her family has given her reasons to live. Her life had no value, and God knew it. While many looked down on her because she was a teen mom, she knew it was the best thing that had ever happened to her. She does not regret it, nor would she ever change it.

Made in the USA
Coppell, TX
16 May 2026

77373382R00095